DATE DUE

DEC 3 0 2010		
NOV 28 2011		
JUL 17 2012		
JUL 27 2012		
APR 0 8 2013		
APR 22 2015		
MAY 20 2015		
SEP 1 7 2015		
OCT 0 8 2015		
MAY 1 3 2016		
JUL 0 5 2018		

Perspectives on Diseases and Disorders

Alzheimer's Disease

Adrienne Wilmoth Lerner and
Alicia Cafferty Lerner
Book Editors

PERSPECTIVES
On Diseases & Disorders

GALE
CENGAGE Learning

Detroit • New York • San Francisco • New Haven, Conn • Waterville, Maine • London

GALE
CENGAGE Learning

Christine Nasso, *Publisher*
Elizabeth Des Chenes, *Managing Editor*

For more information, contact:
Greenhaven Press
27500 Drake Rd.
Farmington Hills, MI 48331-3535
Or you can visit our Internet site at gale.cengage.com

For product information and technology assistance, contact us at

Gale Customer Support, 1-800-877-4253
For permission to use material from this text or product, submit all requests online at www.cengage.com/permissions

Further permissions questions can be emailed to permissionrequest@cengage.com

Articles in Greenhaven Press anthologies are often edited for length to meet page requirements. In addition, original titles of these works are changed to clearly present the main thesis and to explicitly indicate the author's opinion. Every effort is made to ensure that Greenhaven Press accurately reflects the original intent of the authors. Every effort has been made to trace the owners of copyrighted material.

Cover image copyright Dennis Sabo, 2007. Used under license of Shutterstock.com.

LIBRARY OF CONGRESS CATALOGING-IN-PUBLICATION DATA

Alzheimer's disease / Adrienne Wilmoth Lerner, Alicia Cafferty Lerner, book editors.
    p. cm. — (Perspectives on diseases and disorders)
  Includes bibliographical references and index.
  ISBN 978-0-7377-4024-0 (hardcover)
  1. Alzheimer's disease. I. Lerner, Adrienne Wilmoth. II. Lerner, Alicia Cafferty.
  RC523.A37472 2009
  616.8'31—dc22
                                                    2008024351

Printed in the United States of America
  2 3 4 5 6 7 13 12 11 10 09

CONTENTS

CHAPTER 2   Alzheimer's Issues and Controversies

INTRODUCTION

Alzheimer's disease profoundly affects the lives of both patients and caregivers. During the course of the disease, patients require increasing care and assistance. Caregiving evolves from assisting with banking or driving to helping with basic daily tasks such as eating, dressing, and bathing; from periodic visits to round-the-clock care. Since most caregivers are family members, Alzheimer's profoundly affects family life.

In its earliest stages, the first signs of Alzheimer's are often mistaken as normal side effects of aging: forgetfulness, fatigue, diminished interest in regular activities, disorientation, loss of balance, and repetitiveness in conversation.

Few Alzheimer's patients recognize their own symptoms, and many family members only recognize the first signs of Alzheimer's in hindsight, long after their loved one has received a diagnosis. In their most honest moments, many caregiving families will admit to having teased their loved one before diagnosis about "becoming old" or having too many "senior moments."

Families and caregivers are often deeply affected by the diagnosis of Alzheimer's in a loved one. They grapple with sadness and worry about their loved one's future. Since patients often live for many years after diagnosis, families must make plans for an extended period of caregiving that will eventually require full-time care. Many caregiver family members report that soon after being diagnosed with Alzheimer's their loved one entered a period of separation, denial, or resentment toward their future caregivers. Many recently diagnosed Alzheimer's patients worry about becoming a burden to family member caregivers. Some patients experience severe depression.

In the early stages, many Alzheimer's patients are able to live independently. Caregivers assist with complex chores like driving, grocery shopping, banking, and bill paying. They may also ensure that their loved ones remain physically and socially active and that they keep doctors' appointments. When Alzheimer's patients are no longer able to live independently, they are most often cared for by a family member.

Many caregivers report that Alzheimer's patients often revert to childhood memories. (© Phototake Inc./Alamy)

As the disease progresses, memory loss and dementia intensify. The Alzheimer's-afflicted person may have increasing periods during which they are unable to recognize people and are out of touch with reality. Many caregivers report that Alzheimer's patients often revert to childhood memories. They may assert that their parents are expecting them to come home for dinner or mistake their caretaker for a childhood friend. They are more likely to experience periods of disorientation, nervousness about their surroundings, and anger. Some develop wandering habits; others insist on remaining in their room alone.

Caregiver and family life changes substantially to accommodate the loved one with Alzheimer's. Caregivers must ensure that patients eat, groom themselves, and are kept safe. Family schedules change to accommodate meal times and quiet hours that best suit the family member with Alzheimer's. Homes must be altered to prevent falls, rummaging, and accidents. Many caregivers equate these changes to those made to a home with a toddler: cabinets and doors are locked, knick-knacks are cleared from shelves, knives and poisons are kept out of reach, and some furniture is protected or removed.

In addition to the physical changes of the household, many caregiver families experience a change in their social lives. Caregiver families may feel stigmatized by living with someone with Alzheimer's. Children and teens living with an Alzheimer's-afflicted family member often comment that they are embarrassed to have friends in their home. Caregiver families sometimes have difficulty going shopping, visiting with friends, or going to restaurants or movies. Many have been embarrassed in public by the actions of an Alzheimer's-afflicted loved one, even knowing that the patient had no control over those actions. Caregiver families often deal with powerful but conflicting emotions: sadness at their loved one's condition, gratification that they can help a loved one in need, frustration at the social limitations imposed by caregiving, anxiety over financial concerns, and worry that they cannot continue to meet the patient's needs. Caretakers and family members who participate in support groups often learn that other group members share the same emotions, experiences, and concerns.

In the final stages of Alzheimer's, many patients require full-time institutional or at-home professional medical care. At that stage, some family caretakers are comforted by the knowledge that their loved one is getting needed care; others feel guilty that they are unable to provide this level of care themselves. Many caretakers are conflicted, feeling both relieved and sad. For many families, the move to twenty-four-hour care—whether at home or in a facility—signifies the last stages of a long and complex grieving process that begins long before death, a process almost unique to those coping with Alzheimer's. Alzheimer's forces families to suffer loss and grief in stages: when their loved one's personality changes, when they lose touch with the present day, when they fail to recognize the people closest to them, when they begin to fear anyone's touch.

Not all caregiver and family responses are stressful or heartbreaking. Many caregivers assert that taking care of an Alzheimer's-afflicted loved one gives them an intense sense of pride and accomplishment. Many are happy to take care of someone who once took care of them. Others feel that caregiving is a natural part of family life and has instilled family members with a sense of responsibility. Some caregivers report that they gained insights into their Alzheimer's-afflicted parent's childhood and learned his or her deepest fears or most guarded secrets. Some families note that their loved one shared cherished memories and stories soon after being diagnosed with Alzheimer's as a way of preserving them before the disease worsened.

Dealing with Alzheimer's disease is both a deeply personal and a universal experience. Worldwide, more people are being diagnosed with Alzheimer's disease. Cul-

tural, social, and economic conditions affect Alzheimer's care and caregiving. Throughout the world, caregivers are primarily female family members, and most care is provided within the extended family home. In developing regions, this may be the only option for daily care. In spite of differing circumstances, many family experiences with Alzheimer's disease transcend national and cultural boundaries. Alzheimer's caregivers surveyed in over thirty-five nations reported strikingly similar experiences and emotions.

An aging world population and the increasing incidence of Alzheimer's disease make research critical. New drugs have helped Alzheimer's patients live longer and manage symptoms better. Drug regimens combined with therapy can help Alzheimer's-affected persons remain independent longer and can delay the onset of the disease's most severe symptoms, giving patients

In the final stages of Alzheimer's disease, many patients require full-time institutional or at-home professional medical care.
(© Phototake Inc./Alamy)

and families more good days together. However, since so little is known about the disease, there are several current—and sometimes conflicting—theories about how the disease progresses, the best means of prevention and treatment, and who is most likely to develop Alzheimer's. Answering these key questions is essential for improving the lives of Alzheimer's-afflicted people and their families and caregivers.

CHAPTER 1

Understanding Alzheimer's Disease

An Overview of Alzheimer's Disease

Judith Sims, Teresa G. Odle, and Tish Davidson

In the following essay science writers Judith Sims, Teresa G. Odle, and Tish Davidson provide a general overview of the symptoms, possible causes, progression, diagnosis, and treatment of Alzheimer's disease (AD). The authors include a list of warning signs of AD and discuss the drugs approved to treat the symptoms of the disease. They also explore the difficulties of caring for a person with AD and the need to seek outside help to meet the challenges of attending to a patient in the later stages of the disease.

Photo on previous page. French president Nicolas Sarkozy looks through a microscope as he visits the Institute of Molecular and Cellular Pharmacology, in support of the battle against Alzheimer's disease. **(AP Images)**

Alzheimer's disease (AD) is the most common form of dementia, a neurologic disease characterized by loss of mental ability severe enough to interfere with normal activities of daily living, lasting at least six months, and not present from birth. AD usually occurs in old age and is marked by a decline in cognitive functions such as remembering, reasoning, and planning.

SOURCE: Judith Sims, Teresa G. Odle, and Tish Davidson, *The Gale Encyclopedia of Medicine,* Belmont, CA: The Gale Group, 2007. Reproduced by permission of Gale, a part of Cengage Learning.

The Impact of Alzheimer's

German physician Alois Alzheimer first described AD in 1907. The Alzheimer's Association has established seven stages of the disease, ranging from normal and unimpaired to non-responsive. A person with AD usually has a gradual decline in mental functions, often beginning with slight memory loss, followed by losses in the ability to maintain employment, to plan and execute familiar tasks, and to reason and exercise judgment. Communication ability, mood, and personality also may be affected. On average, people who have AD die within eight years of their diagnosis, although the interval is highly variable—as short as one year or as long as 20 years. AD is the fifth leading cause of death in Americans over age 65.

The Alzheimer's Association estimates that in 2007 5.1 million Americans were living with a diagnosis of AD. That number is expected to grow rapidly as the population ages. While a small number of people in their 40s and 50s develop the disease (called early-onset AD), AD predominantly affects the elderly. AD affects about 2% of all people between ages 65 and 74, about 19% of those between 75 and 84, and about 42% of those over 85. This is the equivalent of one of every eight Americans over age 65. Many studies have found that women are at higher risk than men to develop AD. This may be because women tend to live longer, leaving a higher proportion of women in the most affected age groups.

Internationally, in developed countries the rate of AD is about the same as in the United States. In countries such as Japan that have a rapidly aging population, the percentages are higher simply because of the age distribution of the population.

The cost of caring for a person with AD is considerable. The annual cost of caring for one AD patient in 2007 was estimated as about $18,400 for a patient with mild AD, $30,100 for a patient with moderate AD, and $36,100 for a patient with severe AD. The annual costs of caring for AD patients in the United States were estimated to be about $100 billion in 2006. This included both direct patient costs and indirect costs, such as time lost from work by caregivers. On average, Medicare pays more than three times as much for the medical care of a beneficiary with AD as it does for one without AD. Slightly more than half of people with AD are cared for at home, while the remainder are cared for in a variety of health care institutions.

Causes of Alzheimer's

The cause or causes (researchers now believe that there are likely to be multiple causes) of Alzheimer's disease are largely unknown, although some forms of AD have genetic links. Some strong leads have been found through recent research, however, and these have given some theoretical support to several new experimental treatments.

At first AD destroys neurons (nerve cells) in parts of the brain that control memory, including the hippocampus, which is a structure deep in the brain that controls short-term memory. As these neurons in the hippocampus stop functioning, the person's short-term memory fails, and the ability to perform familiar tasks decreases. Later AD affects the cerebral cortex, particularly the areas responsible for language and reasoning. Many language skills are lost and the ability to make judgments is affected. Personality changes occur, which may include emotional outbursts, wandering, and agitation. The severity of these changes increases with disease progression. Eventually many other areas of the brain become involved, the brain regions affected atrophy (shrink and lose function), and the person with AD becomes bedridden, incontinent, helpless, and non-responsive.

Autopsy of a person with AD shows that the regions of the brain affected by the disease become clogged with two abnormal structures, called neurofibrillary tangles and amyloid plaques. Neurofibrillary tangles are twisted masses of protein fibers inside neurons. In AD, tau proteins, which normally help bind and stabilize parts of neurons, are changed chemically, become twisted and tangled, and no longer can stabilize the neurons. Amyloid plaques consist of insoluble deposits of beta-amyloid, a protein fragment from a larger protein called amyloid precursor protein (APP), mixed with parts of neurons and non-nerve cells. Plaques are found in the spaces between the nerve cells of the brain.

While it is not clear exactly how these structures cause problems, many researchers believe that their formation is responsible for the mental changes of AD, presumably

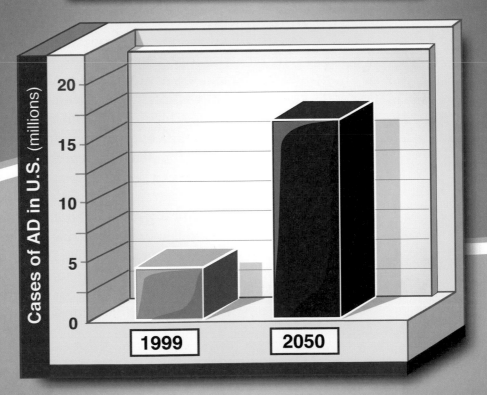

Projected Number of Alzheimer's Cases in the United States

Cases of AD in U.S. (millions)

1999

2050

Taken from: National Institutes of Health, 2002.

by interfering with the normal communication between neurons in the brain and later leading to the death of neurons. As of 2007, the United States Food and Drug Administration (FDA) approved five prescription drugs for the treatment of AD symptoms. Four of these are used to treat mild to moderate AD. They are galantamine (Razadyne formerly known as Reminyl), rivastigmine (Exelon), donepezil (Aricept), and tacrine (Cognex). These drugs all act by increasing the level of chemical signaling molecules (neurotransmitters) in the brain to help compensate for decreased communication ability among nerve cells. The fifth drug, memantine (Namenda), is used to treat moderate to severe AD. It acts by regulating a chemical in the brain called glutamate. None of these drugs cure or stop AD. In some individuals, they do slow the progression of symptoms by modestly increasing cognition and improving the individual's ability to perform normal activities of daily living. Treatment of AD is an active research area. Clinical trials of new drugs and therapies are underway. . . .

Exactly what triggers the formation of plaques and tangles and the development of AD is unknown. AD likely results from many interrelated factors, including genetic, environmental, and others not yet identified. Two types of AD exist: familial AD (FAD), which is a rare autosomal dominant inherited disease, and sporadic AD, with no obvious inheritance pattern. AD also is described in terms of age at onset, with early-onset AD occurring in people younger than 65, and late-onset occurring in those 65 and older. Early-onset AD comprises less than 7% of AD cases and affects people aged 30–60. Some, but not all, cases of early-onset AD are inherited and run in families. Early-onset AD often progresses faster than the more common late-onset type.

As many as half of FAD cases are believed to be caused by three genes located on three different chromosomes. . . .

FAST FACT

Every seventy-two seconds, someone in the United States develops Alzheimer's disease.

There is no evidence that the mutated genes that cause early-onset FAD also cause late-onset AD, but genetics also appears to play a role in this more common form of AD. . . .

Other non-genetic factors have been studied in relation to the causes of AD. Inflammation of the brain may play a role in development of AD. Taking nonsteroidal anti-inflammatory drugs (NSAIDs) was at one time thought to reduce the risk of developing AD. The hoped-for protective effect of NSAIDs has since been disproved through a large, well-controlled clinical trial. Other agents once thought to reduce chances of dementia are now thought to increase its risk. In 2002, hormone replacement therapy (HRT), which combines estrogen and progestogen, was found to double the risk of developing dementia in postmenopausal women.

While the ultimate cause or causes of Alzheimer's disease are unknown, several risk factors increase a person's likelihood of developing the disease. The most significant one is age; older people develop AD at much higher rates than younger ones. There is some evidence that strokes and AD may be linked, with small strokes that go undetected clinically contributing to the injury of neurons. A 2003 Dutch study reported that symptomless, unnoticed strokes could double the risk of AD and other dementias. Blood cholesterol levels also may be important. Scientists have shown that high blood cholesterol levels in special breeds of genetically engineered (transgenic) mice may increase the rate of plaque deposition. There are also parallels between AD and other progressive neurodegenerative disorders that cause dementia, including prion diseases, Parkinson's disease, and Huntington's disease. . . .

Symptoms of Alzheimer's

The symptoms of Alzheimer's disease begin gradually, usually with memory lapses. Occasional memory lapses are common to everyone and do not by themselves signify any change in cognitive function. The person with AD may begin with only the routine sort of memory lapse—forgetting where the car keys are—but progress to more profound or disturbing losses, such as forgetting that he or she can drive a car. Becoming lost or disoriented on a walk around the neighborhood becomes more likely as the disease progresses. A person with AD may forget the names of family members or forget what was said at the beginning of a sentence by the time he hears the end.

As AD progresses, other symptoms appear, including inability to perform routine tasks, loss of judgment, and personality or behavior changes. Some people with AD have trouble sleeping and may experience confusion or agitation in the evening ("sunsetting" or Sundowner's Syndrome). In some cases, people with AD repeat the same ideas, movements, words, or thoughts. In the final stages people may have severe problems with eating, communicating, and controlling their bladder and bowel functions.

The Alzheimer's Association has developed a list of 10 warning signs of AD. A person with several of these symptoms should see a physician for a thorough evaluation:

- memory loss that affects job skills
- difficulty performing familiar tasks
- problems with language
- disorientation of time and place
- poor or decreased judgment
- problems with abstract thinking
- misplacing things
- changes in mood or behavior
- changes in personality
- loss of initiative

Other types of dementia, including some that are reversible, can cause similar symptoms. A person with some of the symptoms listed above should be evaluated by a professional who can weigh the possibility that his or her symptoms may have another cause. Approximately 20% of individuals originally suspected of having AD turn out to have some other disorder; about half of these cases are treatable.

Diagnosing Alzheimer's

Diagnosis of Alzheimer's disease is complex, and may require office visits to several different specialists over several months before a diagnosis can be made. While a confident provisional diagnosis may be made in most cases after thorough testing, AD cannot be diagnosed definitively until autopsy examination of the brain for plaques and neurofibrillary tangles.

The diagnosis of AD begins with a thorough physical exam and complete medical history. An accurate history of symptoms from family members or caregivers is essential because impaired cognition makes it difficult for the individual with AD to provide accurate information. Since there are both prescription and over-the-counter drugs that can cause the same mental changes as AD, a careful review of the patient's drug, medicine, and alcohol use is important. AD-like symptoms also can be associated with other medical conditions, including tumors, infection, and dementia caused by mild strokes (multi-infarct dementia). These possibilities must be ruled out as well through appropriate blood and urine tests, brain magnetic resonance imaging (MRI), positron emission tomography (PET) or single photon emission computed tomography (SPECT) scans, tests of the brain's electrical activity (electroencephalographs or EEGs), or other tests. Several types of oral and written tests are used to aid in the AD diagnosis and to follow its progression, including tests of mental status, functional abilities, memory, and concentration. Still, the neurologic exam is normal in most patients in early stages.

One of the most important parts of the diagnostic process is to evaluate the patient for depression and delirium, since each of these can be present with AD, or may be mistaken for it. (Delirium involves a decreased consciousness or awareness of one's environment.) Depression and memory loss both are common in the elderly, and the combination of them often can be mistaken for AD. Depression can be treated with drugs, although some antidepressants can worsen dementia if it is present, further complicating both diagnosis and treatment.

An early and accurate diagnosis of AD is important in developing strategies for managing symptoms and for helping patients and their families plan for the future and to allow them to pursue care options while the patient can still take part in the decision-making process.

A genetic test for the APOE e4 gene [which is linked to Alzheimer's disease] is available, but is not used for diagnosis, since possessing even two copies of this gene does not ensure that a person will develop AD. In addition, access to genetic information could affect the insurability, employment status, and legal rights of a patient if disclosed.

Treatment of Alzheimer's

Alzheimer's disease is presently incurable. As noted above, as of 2007, five drugs were approved for treating AD. These may slow, but not reverse or stop symptoms. Starting drug treatment as early as possible in the course of AD can help people with the disease maintain independent function as long as possible. The remaining treatment for a person with AD is good nursing care and providing both physical and emotional support for a person who is gradually able to do less and less for himself and whose behavior is becoming more and more erratic. Modifications of the home to increase safety and security often are necessary. The caregiver also needs support to prevent anger, despair, and burnout from becoming overwhelming. Becoming familiar with the issues likely to lie ahead, and considering the appropriate financial

German physician Alois Alzheimer (1864–1915) first documented "presenile dementia" in 1907. (**Photo Researchers, Inc.**)

and legal issues early on, can help both the patient and family cope with the difficult process of the disease. Regular medical care by a practitioner with a non-defeatist attitude toward AD is important, so that illnesses such as urinary or respiratory infections can be diagnosed and treated properly, rather than being incorrectly attributed to the inevitable decline seen in AD.

People with AD often are depressed or anxious and may suffer from sleeplessness, poor nutrition, and general poor health. Each of these conditions is treatable to some degree. It is important for the person with AD to eat well and continue to exercise. Professional advice from a nutritionist may be useful to provide healthy, easy-to-prepare meals. Finger foods may be preferable to foods requiring utensils to be eaten. Regular exercise (supervised if necessary for safety) promotes overall health. A calm, structured environment with simple orientation aids, such as calendars and clocks, may reduce anxiety and increase safety. Other psychiatric symptoms, such as depression, anxiety, hallucinations (seeing or hearing things that are not there), and delusions (false beliefs), may be treated with drugs if necessary. Drugs such as antidepressants, anti-psychotics, and sedatives are also used to treat the behavioral symptoms, such as agitation, aggression, wandering, and sleep disorders. Research is being conducted to search for better treatments, including non-drug approaches for AD patients.

Nursing Care and Safety

The person with Alzheimer's disease will gradually lose the ability to dress, groom, feed, bathe, or use the toilet by himself; in the later stages of the disease, he may be unable to move or speak. In addition, the person's behavior becomes increasingly erratic. A tendency to wander may make it difficult to leave an AD patient unattended for even a few minutes and make the home a potentially dangerous place. In addition, some people with AD may exhibit inappropriate sexual behaviors.

The nursing care required for a person with AD is well within the abilities of most people to learn. The difficulty for many caregivers comes in the constant, but unpredictable, nature of the demands put on them. In addition, the personality changes undergone by a person with AD can be heartbreaking for family members as a loved one deteriorates, seeming to become a different person. Not all people with AD develop negative behaviors. Some become quite gentle, and spend increasing amounts of time in dreamlike states.

A loss of good grooming may be one of the early symptoms of AD. Mismatched clothing, unkempt hair, and decreased interest in personal hygiene become more common. Caregivers, especially spouses, may find these changes socially embarrassing and difficult to cope with. The caregiver usually will need to spend increasing amounts of time on grooming to compensate for the loss of attention from the patient, although some adjustment of expectations (while maintaining cleanliness) is often needed as the disease progresses. . . .

Persons with dementia must deal with six basic safety concerns: injury from falls, injury from ingesting dangerous substances, leaving the home and getting lost, injury to self or others from sharp objects, fire or burns, and the inability to respond rapidly to crisis situations. In all cases, a person diagnosed with AD should no longer be allowed to drive, because of the increased potential for accidents and the increased likelihood of wandering very far from home while disoriented. In the home, simple measures such as grab bars in the bathroom, bed rails on the bed, and easily negotiable passageways can greatly increase safety. Electrical appliances should be unplugged and put away when not in use, and matches, lighters, knives, or weapons should be stored safely out of reach. The hot water heater temperature may be lowered to prevent accidental scalding. A list of emergency numbers, including the poison control center and the hospital emergency room, should be posted by the telephone. As the disease progresses, caregivers need to periodically reevaluate the physical safety of the home and introduce new strategies for continued safety. . . .

Seeking Outside Help

Most families eventually need outside help to relieve some of the burden of around-the-clock care for a person with AD. Personal care assistants, either volunteer or paid, may be available through local social service agencies.

Adult daycare facilities are becoming increasingly common. Meal delivery, shopping assistance, or respite care may be available as well.

Providing the total care required by a person with late-stage AD can become an overwhelming burden for a family, even with outside help. At this stage, many families consider nursing home care. This decision often is one of the most difficult for the family, since it is often seen as an abandonment of the loved one and a failure of the family. Careful counseling with a sympathetic physician, clergy, or other trusted adviser may ease the difficulties of this transition. Selecting a nursing home may require a difficult balancing of cost, services, location, and availability. Keeping the entire family involved in the decision may help prevent further stress from developing later on.

The Relationship Between Diet and Alzheimer's Disease

National Institute on Aging, Alzheimer's Disease Education & Referral Center

Researchers have long emphasized the connection between a healthy diet and an individual's overall health. However, less is known about how the components of one's diet, such as particular foods or daily intake of certain vitamins, affect an individual's risk of disease. The following article from the U.S. National Institute on Aging discusses a 2002 study that suggests that a diet rich in foods containing vitamin E may reduce the risk of Alzheimer's disease (AD). The study found that vitamin E supplements—as opposed to vitamin E occurring naturally in foods—were not associated with a reduced risk of AD. The authors note the difficulties of studying the effects of vitamins, the possible significance of differences in participant lifestyles, and the need for further study. The National Institute on Aging is part of the National Institutes of Health, the primary U.S. government agency responsible for biomedical research.

SOURCE: National Institute on Aging, "Diet Rich in Foods with Vitamin E May Reduce Alzheimer's Disease Risk," Alzheimer's Disease Education & Referral Center, 2002.

A new population-based study of antioxidants, appearing in the June 26, 2002, *Journal of the American Medical Association* (*JAMA*), suggests that a diet rich in foods containing vitamin E may help protect some people against Alzheimer's disease (AD). The study is also noteworthy for its finding that vitamin E in the form of supplements was not associated with a reduction in the risk of AD. The latest in a series of reports on vitamin E and dementia, the study findings heighten interest in the outcome of clinical trials now underway to test the effectiveness of vitamin E and other antioxidants in preventing or postponing cognitive decline and AD.

The *JAMA* study was conducted by Martha Clare Morris, Sc.D., of the Rush Institute for Healthy Aging at Rush-Presbyterian-St. Luke's Medical Center, Chicago, IL, Denis A. Evans, M.D., and colleagues. A related study by Morris and colleagues . . . in the July 2002 *Archives of Neurology*, a *JAMA* publication, also associates vitamin E with protection against more general cognitive decline. . . . Both studies were supported by the National Institute on Aging (NIA) at the National Institutes of Health.

The June 26 issue of *JAMA* includes similar findings from scientists in The Netherlands, who also reported a link between high dietary intake of vitamins C and E and protection against AD in certain people. In addition, the journal contains an editorial on the epidemiological study of dietary intake of antioxidants and the risk of AD by Daniel J. Foley, M.S., of the NIA's Laboratory of Epidemiology, Demography, and Biometry, and Lon White, M.D., Pacific Health Research Institute, Honolulu.

"This and a number of important population studies have pointed to vitamin E as possibly protective against oxidative damage or other mechanisms associated with cognitive decline and dementia," says Neil Buckholtz, Ph.D., head of the Dementias of Aging Branch at the NIA. "The only way this association can really be tested is through

A number of studies examine the possible importance of vitamin E as protection against Alzheimer's disease in certain people. (**Eric Schrempp/Photo Researchers, Inc.**)

clinical studies and trials now underway. These will help us determine whether vitamin E in food or in supplements— or taken together—can prevent or slow down the development of mild cognitive impairment or AD."

High Doses of Vitamin E Are Not Recommended

It is not recommended, based on current evidence, that people take high-dose vitamin E supplements or other antioxidant pills in an effort to prevent mental decline, Buckholtz says. While population-based studies and animal research have suggested that antioxidants may

Projected Alzheimer's Numbers Across the United States

This table shows the projected number and percent change in people 65+ with Alzheimer's disease between 2000 and 2010, by state.

State	2000	2010	% change
Colorado	49,000	72,000	47
District of Columbia	10,000	9,100	–9
Florida	360,000	450,000	25
Missouri	110,000	110,000	0
Nevada	21,000	29,000	38
New York	330,000	320,000	–3
North Carolina	130,000	170,000	31
Oregon	57,000	76,000	33
Tennessee	100,000	120,000	20
Texas	270,000	340,000	26
Utah	22,000	32,000	45
Washington	83,000	110,000	33

Taken from: "State-specific Projections Through 2025 of Alzheimer's Disease Prevalence," *Neurology*, 2004.

be neuroprotective, clinical trials to test that notion are currently in progress. Little is known about safety, effectiveness, and dosages of various antioxidant supplements that are proposed for neuroprotective purposes, Buckholtz emphasizes.

In excessively high doses (above 2,000 International Units daily, or IU/d), for example, vitamin E may be associated with increased risk of bleeding, and patients taking anti-coagulant medications may be especially at risk. Interactions with other medications commonly taken by older people are also of potential concern. People are advised to consult with their physicians before taking high doses of supplemental vitamin E or other antioxidants.

Studying Vitamins, Diet, and Alzheimer's Risk

The 815 people participating in the Morris study were part of the Chicago Health and Aging Project (CHAP), a study of a large, diverse community of people age 65 and older. Participants were free of dementia at the start of the study and followed for an average of 3.9 years. At an average of 1.7 years from their baseline assessment, participants completed a questionnaire, asking them in detail about the kinds and quantities of foods consumed in the previous year.

Some 131 participants had been diagnosed with AD by the end of the study period, when researchers examined the relationship between intake of antioxidants, including dietary and supplemental vitamins E and C, beta carotene, and a multivitamin, and development of AD. The most significant protective effect was found among people in the top fifth of dietary vitamin E intake (averaging 11.4 IU/d), whose risk of AD was 67 percent lower when compared to people in the group with the lowest vitamin E consumption from food (averaging 6.2 IU/d). (The recommended dietary allowance of vitamin E is 22 IU/d.)

> ## FAST FACT
>
> September 21 is World Alzheimer's Day, set aside by Alzheimer's associations around the world to concentrate on raising awareness about dementia.

Taking Many Factors into Account

No significant change in risk of AD was found when the scientists looked at vitamin E supplements, the other antioxidants and their supplements, or a general multivitamin. There was some evidence, though not statistically significant, that increased intake of dietary vitamin C and beta carotene was moving in a "protective direction," the researchers said.

The data were also analyzed to see if age, gender, race, education, or possible genetic risk for AD would influence the findings. Only the presence or lack of apoE-4, one form of a protein associated with increased risk of late-onset AD, seemed to matter, the protective effect of vitamin E from food was strongest among people who did not have the apoE-4 risk factor allele. "Dietary vitamin E may protect against Alzheimer's disease," says Morris, "but the protection may only occur among people without the apoE-4 allele."

Morris suggests that further study in key areas is needed to confirm and explain some of the study's findings, including the link with apoE status and the study's striking distinction between dietary intake of vitamin E and use of supplements. For example, the lack of a protective effect for the supplements could be explained by several factors.

Some participants in the study started taking supplements only recently and there may not have been sufficient time for the supplement to be found effective. Also, people who believe they have memory problems could be more likely to take the supplements in the first place. Another possible explanation might be variations in the forms of vitamin E, scientists note. Most vitamin E supplements consist of alpha tocopherol while foods are generally more rich in gamma tocopherol.

These forms of vitamin E scavenge different types of free radicals, with one possibly more important than another in potentially reducing risk of cognitive decline. To help determine whether vitamin E might play a role in preventing AD, or at least in delaying its onset, a number of clinical trials are now being supported by the NIA.

Researching the Origins of Alzheimer's Disease

Sue Halpern

In the following viewpoint Sue Halpern describes the work of neurologist and epidemiologist Richard Mayeux. Mayeux and his research team have been studying the prevalence of Alzheimer's disease (AD) among Dominican families in the Dominican Republic and in New York City. The team compiles genealogical and clinical data on the occurrence of AD within families to supplement collaborative research on genetics and AD. The researchers interact with patients, family members, and caregivers, sometimes traveling thousands of miles to study families affected by Alzheimer's. Their goal is to uncover the genes that increase the risk of contracting Alzheimer's in the hope that such a discovery may one day lead to a cure. Halpern writes for *Slate*, the *New Yorker*, and the *New York Times*. She has written several books, including a work on memory research.

One morning last May in the Dominican Republic, two white S.U.V.s left the parking garage at the Gran Almirante Hotel and Casino, in Santiago, just as the gamblers and prostitutes were calling it a night, and headed half an hour north, to the town of Navarette. The lead vehicle was driven by Angel Piriz, a thirty-seven-year-old Cuban doctor who lives in New York. Beside him was Rosarina Estevez, a recent graduate of medical school in Santiago. Both were working as research physicians at Columbia University under the supervision of Richard Mayeux. For nearly twenty years, Mayeux, a neurologist, epidemiologist, and the director of the Taub Institute for Research on Alzheimer's Disease and the Aging Brain, has been compiling the world's most comprehensive genetic library of families with Alzheimer's, in an effort to uncover the biological origins of a disease that affects 4.5 million Americans. The family members are predominantly residents of the heavily Dominican neighborhood of Washington Heights, where the Taub Institute is based, or, like the family that the Columbia researchers were hoping to see, from the Dominican Republic itself.

Navarette isn't much of a town—a strip of concrete shops on either side of the road, and street venders selling pineapples and mangoes and fresh goat meat—and the family didn't have much of an address. "It's called Ginger Alley," Vincent Santana, the driver of the second vehicle, said, turning sharply into a narrow dirt track patrolled by chickens. Santana, who is in charge of the researchers' field work, gathered the notebooks and questionnaires they would need to administer the neuropsychological tests that, along with a medical exam, would determine who would be given a diagnosis of Alzheimer's disease.

Hunting for the Alzheimer's Genes

Alzheimer's can be divided into two categories. One is known as early-onset Alzheimer's, which is rare, and tends to strike between the ages of thirty and sixty. Almost half of early-onset Alzheimer's is straightforwardly genetic, and follows the simple laws of Mendelian inheritance: if you are born with the mutated gene, you get the disease. Much

Change in Selected Leading Causes of Death in the United States, 2000–2004

Cause	2000	2004	% change
Heart disease	710,760	654,092	−8.0
Breast cancer	41,200	40,110	−2.6
Prostate cancer	31,900	29,900	−6.3
Stroke	167,661	150,147	−10.4
Alzheimer's disease	49,558	65,829	+32.8

Taken from: Centers for Disease Control and Prevention, National Vital Statistics Reports, and Reports of the American Cancer Society.

more common is the late-onset disease, which tends to afflict people who are sixty-five and older. Because the prevalence of late-onset Alzheimer's increases as the population ages, the number of cases is expected to double in the next twenty-five years. Late-onset Alzheimer's is thought to be genetically influenced, too, but in a much less predictable way: it appears to involve perhaps half a dozen genes that, individually or in combination, increase one's risk of dementia. Researchers all over the world have spent the past decade hunting for these risk-factor genes, spurred by the impending public-health crisis and the daunting insufficiency of available treatments. They believe that working out the genetics of late-onset Alzheimer's, and thus finding molecular pathways that influence the course of the disease, was the best—and possibly the only—hope for finding a cure. So far, only one of those risk-factor genes has been conclusively identified. In May, though, as the Columbia researchers travelled through the Dominican Republic, drawing blood that was sent by FedEx each day to New York, it looked as if Mayeux's library might soon yield a second. . . .

As the researchers walked through the neighborhood, they attracted a parade of young boys, who eventually led them to Vargas's house, a spare, three-room dwelling. Vargas, a gaunt eighty-three-year-old who was tanned from a life growing bananas and tending rice fields, was lying, bare-chested and wearing blue shorts, on a bed with yellow smiley-face sheets. Surrounded by two of his five wives, four of his fourteen children, and an assortment of other relatives, he wasn't saying much. . . .

FAST FACT

As of 2006, more than 60 percent of people with dementia live in developing countries, but by 2040 this will rise to 71 percent. China, India, and the nations of south Asia and the western Pacific have some of the fastest-growing elderly populations.

Santana had known about Vargas for almost a year. In his notes from an interview with the proband [the first person in the family that Mayeux's team saw] in the spring of 2004, there was a reminder to identify and track down all her cousins and their siblings, in order to determine how they were related. Constructing accurate genealogies, which is what Santana does, is fundamental to figuring out how a disease travels among kin, which is what Richard Mayeux does.

"What day of the week is it?" Santana asked Vargas. A series of questions followed: "What is the date?" "What year?" "Where are we?" This was the warmup, and Vargas was doing O.K. He knew that he was in the bedroom, not the kitchen; he knew the year; he knew the season.

Santana leaned in close. "I'm going to read you a list of twelve words, and when I'm done I want you to repeat them back to me. *Huevo*," he began. "*Lava*." Vargas fingered a religious medal he wore around his neck and looked lost. "I can't remember," he said, pointing to his head. The verbal test is one part of a forty-five-minute battery of exams that was developed for the Dominican Republic study by Yaakov Stern, a neuropsychologist who has worked with Mayeux for more than twenty years. If someone, given the opportunity to repeat any of the twelve words six times, for a top score of seventy-two, can't get to twenty-five, he might be considered for "case status." When the test was over, Vargas's score was well below that.

In the next room, Piriz was going through the same routine with one of Vargas's wives, a short seventy-year-old woman in a faded housedress and flip-flops, who was eying him warily. "Do you ever find yourself getting lost?" Piriz asked. "Hell no," she said. He took her blood pressure, looked into her eyes, tested her reflexes. Then he put on green latex gloves, took out a syringe, and prepared to draw her blood.

Making the Genetic Connection

"I started off thinking Alzheimer's was not a genetic disease," Mayeux told me the first time I visited him, last November, in his unusually tidy office, on the nineteenth floor of the Presbyterian Hospital Building, on West 168th Street. "I thought it was environmental, associated with aging. But the accumulating data convinced me. It doesn't always follow a pattern, but it does also track in families, so that if you have family members with the disease you have a much higher risk of getting it, and siblings with the disease give you an even higher risk. The evidence was very hard to counter." . . .

"What we wanted to do was find a population where we thought the rates were higher, because the thing about genetics is that if you try to identify people who carry the gene you are looking for unusual people," Mayeux said. "It's not like epidemiology, where you try to get random samples of random people. Genetics is just the opposite. You want a biased population. You want families where there is more of the disease, because you have a better chance of figuring out what the gene is.

"That's how we stumbled into this study of people in the Dominican Republic," he went on. "We noticed, when we were doing a general population study of elderly people who live around the hospital, that Dominicans had about three times the rate of Alzheimer's disease compared to the whites in the community. So you have to ask yourself why that would be. Then it starts to explain itself that, at least in the Dominican Republic, Dominicans tend to marry other Dominicans, and you don't have different populations moving in there. You have a smaller genetic pool, and the gene pool tends to stay enriched." . . .

The members of Mayeux's team had no illusions about what real progress would require. They were looking for mutated genes, for corrupted molecular pathways, for predictors of disease, for effective therapies. The search was painstaking, fraught, and more prone to failure than to success; it was also exhilarating. . . .

The Complexity of Genetic Puzzles

There's a simple reason that no one has found a new Alzheimer's gene in more than a decade, and another reason that is less simple, and they both come down to the same thing: statistics. Risk-factor genes, the genes that will explain late-onset Alzheimer's, are inherently elusive, because carrying them does not automatically presage disease. More challenging, there may be many risk-factor genes, each with a potentially minute effect. To detect such genes requires a large, geographically isolated family study like Mayeux's, with reams of information about each individual's health issues, eating habits, and work and leisure pursuits, as well as genealogies that show the genetic path of the disease. Mayeux's thick books of pedigrees and his database of DNA allow researchers to define a person's genotype (what genes she carries) as well as a phenotype (what traits she embodies) and then to subdivide the phenotype according to which traits specifically correlate with the kind of dementia that characterizes Alzheimer's disease. On the nineteenth floor of the Presbyterian Hospital Building, the crucial diagnostic marker seemed to be a person's performance on certain memory tests, and the researchers were seeing a pattern in performance and disease which they hoped would show up in the genes.

"Age of onset is a wimpy phenotype," Mayeux said to no one in particular at one of the team's weekly genetics meetings in his office earlier this year. Mayeux thought that relying on family members to identify when a subject began showing signs of the disease was too subjective. "Memory is better. It's quantifiable."

"Delayed recognition is the most sensitive test we have for A.D. [Alzheimer's disease]" Joe Lee, the geneticist, told him. "That and another test that I can't recall. I may be a subject for this study soon myself."

A speech therapist tests a patient at home for Alzheimer's disease. (Mendil/Photo Researchers, Inc.)

"We all may be," Mayeux said, laughing. It is a measure of the disease's prevalence that the seven people sitting around the table had a mother, a father, an aunt, a grandmother, and a grandfather with Alzheimer's. . . .

Mayeux thinks that, a decade from now, your doctor will look up your gene profile and decide whether you have a high risk for Alzheimer's, and then give you a prophylactic treatment of some sort. "Right now, you don't know what the hell to do," Mayeux said . . . "You don't know whether you should take vitamins, whether you should take ibuprofen, and, if you do, if you'll get a stroke, whether you should take estrogen, and if that will give you a stroke. People tell you to use your brain, to use your body, and those are all well and good, but you don't know if it's a lifetime of doing those things, you don't know if it's starting to do crosswords when you're ninety. If we can solve some of these genetic puzzles, we'll know how to treat the disease."

Diagnosing Alzheimer's Disease

University of Maryland Medical Center

Often patients must be observed for several months before doctors can provisionally diagnose Alzheimer's disease. Many Alzheimer's symptoms are similar to those of other diseases or are more difficult to diagnose in elderly patients, the group most at risk of developing Alzheimer's. Loved ones and caregivers are often the first to recognize a patient's Alzheimer's-related symptoms. The following article from the University of Maryland Medical Center discusses possible symptoms of Alzheimer's and the process of clinically diagnosing the disease.

A definitive test to diagnose Alzheimer's disease, even in patients showing signs of dementia, has not yet been developed. A number of expert groups have developed criteria to help diagnose Alzheimer's disease and rule out other disorders. A diagnosis often involves answering questions about the patient:

- Do psychologic tests indicate dementia?
- Does the patient have deficits in two or more areas of mental functioning (such as language, motor skills, and perceptions)?
- Have memory and mental functions gotten progressively worse?
- Is consciousness disturbed? (It is not in Alzheimer's disease.)
- Is the patient over age 40?
- Are other medical or physical conditions present that could account for the same symptoms?
- Is daily activity impaired or has the behavior changed?
- Is there a family history of Alzheimer's disease?
- Are there other symptoms, such as depression, insomnia, incontinence, delusions, hallucinations, dramatic verbal, emotional or physical outbursts, sexual disorders, and weight loss?

Other steps involved in making a decision include laboratory tests (EEG and possibly tests to rule out other diseases) and psychological testing to determine the presence of dementia.

Ruling Out Conditions of Normal Aging

Although some memory impairment occurs in many people as they age, only some of these people develop Alzheimer's disease. Many similar symptoms can occur in healthy older individuals from other conditions associated with aging:

- Fatigue
- Grief or depression
- Illness
- Vision or hearing loss
- The use of alcohol or certain medications
- Simply the burden of too many details to remember at once

Ruling Out Other Causes of Memory Loss or Dementia

The first step in diagnosing Alzheimer's disease is to rule out other conditions that might cause memory loss or dementia. There are a number of causes for dementia in the elderly besides Alzheimer's disease:

- Vascular dementia (abnormalities in the vessels that carry blood to the brain)
- Lewy bodies variant (LBV), also called dementia with Lewy bodies
- Parkinson's disease
- Frontotemporal dementia

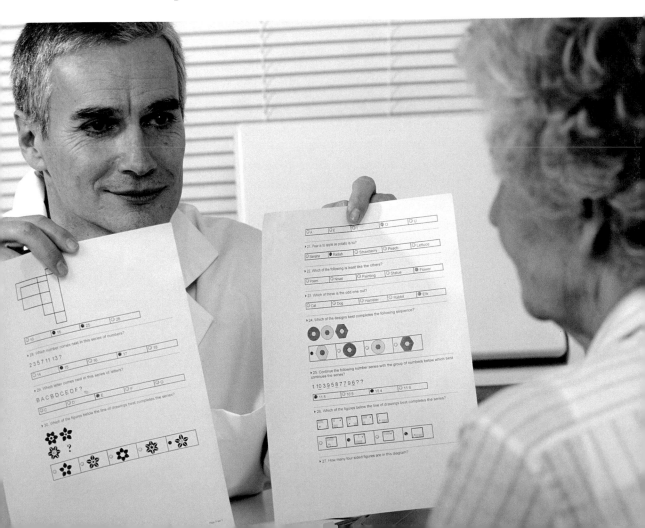

Psychological testing is one of a battery of tests given to patients to help diagnose Alzheimer's disease. (**BSIP/Photo Researchers, Inc.**)

Experts believe that 60% of cases of dementia are due to Alzheimer's, 15% to vascular injuries, and the rest are a mixture of the two or caused by other factors.

Vascular Dementia. Vascular dementia is primarily caused by either multi-infarct dementia (multiple small strokes) or Binswanger's disease (which affects tiny arteries in the midbrain). One major analysis suggested that patients with vascular dementia have better long term verbal memory than patients with Alzheimer's disease, but poorer executive function (less ability to integrate and organize).

Lewy Bodies Variant. Lewy bodies are abnormalities found in the brains of patients with both Parkinson's disease and Alzheimer's. They can also be present in the absence of either disease; in such cases, the condition is called Lewy bodies variant (LBV). In all cases, the presence of Lewy bodies is highly associated with dementia. LBV was defined in 1997 and some experts believe it may be responsible for about 20% of people who have been diagnosed with Alzheimer's. They can be difficult to distinguish. Compared to Alzheimer's disease patients, those with LBV may be more likely to have hallucinations and delusions early on, to walk with a stoop (similar to Parkinson's disease), to have more fluctuating attention problems, and to perform better than Alzheimer's disease patients on verbal recall but less well with organizing objects.

Parkinson's Disease. Dementia is about six times more common in the elderly Parkinson's patient than in the average older adult. It is most likely to occur in older patients who have had major depression. Unlike in Alzheimer's, language is not usually affected in Parkinson's related dementia. Visual hallucinations occur in about a third of people on long-term medications.

Parkinson's disease is a slowly progressive disorder that affects movement, muscle control, and balance. Part of the disease process develops as cells are destroyed in

FAST FACT

The direct and indirect costs of Alzheimer's and other dementias amount to more than $148 billion annually.

certain parts of the brain stem, particularly the crescent-shaped cell mass known as the substantia nigra. Nerve cells in the substantia nigra send out fibers to tissue located in both sides of the brain. There the cells release essential neurotransmitters that help control movement and coordination.

Frontotemporal Dementia (FTD). Once considered rare, FTD is now considered to be the second most common cause of early-onset dementia. People who develop this condition tend to be in their mid-fifties although it can develop later on. It results in greater behavioral impairment (apathy, reduced empathy, poor self-care, unrestrained behavior) than with Alzheimer's disease. It may also be marked by speech problems and early incontinence. Brain imaging scans can help diagnose this problem.

Other Conditions that Cause Similar Symptoms. Some elderly people have a condition called mild cognitive impairment, which involves more severe memory loss than normal but no other symptoms of Alzheimer's. A number of conditions, including many medications, can produce symptoms similar to Alzheimer's:

- Severe depression
- Drug abuse
- Thyroid disease
- Severe vitamin B12 deficiency
- Blood clots
- Hydrocephalus (excessive accumulation of spinal fluid in the brain)
- Syphilis
- Huntington's disease
- Creutzfeldt-Jakob disease
- Brain tumors

It is important that the doctor recognize any treatable conditions that might be causing symptoms or worsening existing dementia caused by Alzheimer's or vascular abnormalities.

Psychological Testing

A number of psychologic tests are used or being developed to assess difficulties in attention, perception, and memory and problem-solving, social, and language skills. Experts are researching specific tests that may help identify early on people with mild memory impairment who are at high risk for Alzheimer's disease.

- Two commonly used tests that are very useful in identifying individuals who may be at risk for Alzheimer's are the Mini-Mental State Exam (MMSE) and the Mattis Dementia Rating Scale. Still, these tests have limitations.

- A clock drawing test is also a good test for Alzheimer's disease. The patient is given a piece of paper with a circle on it and is first asked to write the numbers in the face of a clock and then to show "10 minutes after 11." The score is based on spacing between the numbers and the positions of the hands.

Electroencephalography

Electroencephalography (EEG) traces brain-wave activity; in some patients with Alzheimer's disease this test reveals "slow waves." Although other diseases may evidence similar abnormalities, EEG data helps distinguish a potential patient with Alzheimer's disease from a patient with severe depression, whose brain waves are normal.

Imaging Tests

Imaging tests include magnetic resonance imaging (MRI), positron-emission tomography (PET), and single photon emission computed tomography (SPECT). These tests are sometimes used to rule out other disorders such as multi-infarct dementia, stroke, blood clots, and tumors.

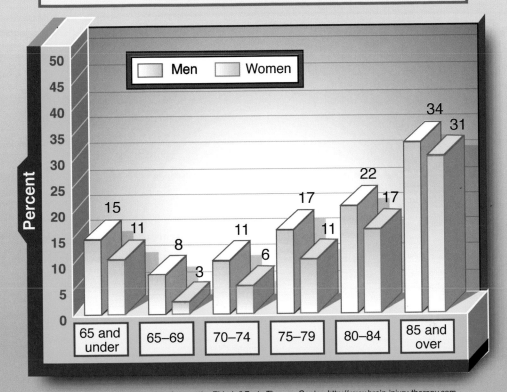

Moderate or Severe Memory Impairment

This 2002 graph shows the percentage of people age 65 and over with moderate or severe memory impairment. The definition of "moderate or severe memory impairment" is four or fewer words recalled (out of twenty) on combined immediate and delayed recall tests among self-respondents.

Men **Women**

Percent

Age	Men	Women
65 and under	15	11
65–69	8	3
70–74	11	6
75–79	17	11
80–84	22	17
85 and over	34	31

Taken from: "Cognitive Disorders Among the Elderly," Brain Therapy Center. http://www.brain-injury-therapy.com.

Research is being conducted to determine if these tests can help to confirm a diagnosis of Alzheimer's disease and improve understanding of disease progression.

In 2005, the National Institute of Aging, in collaboration with industry partners, launched the $60 million Alzheimer's Disease Neuroimaging Initiative (ADNI). This landmark 5-year clinical trial, which will be conducted at 50 sites throughout the United States and Canada, will investigate whether neuroimaging techniques, such as MRI and PET scans, can be combined with biomarkers and neuropsychological tests to measure the progression of AD and mild cognitive impairment. In 2004, the U.S. Medicare system expanded insurance coverage of PET scans for eligible beneficiaries who meet specific diagnostic criteria for both Alzheimer's disease and frontotemporal dementia. Medicare also covers the costs for patients enrolled in its agency-approved imaging clinical trials.

Research continues on Pittsburgh compound B, a tracer molecule used in PET brain scans to highlight beta-amyloid protein deposits. Results from this research may help to define potential drug targets and aid in the development of new Alzheimer's drugs.

Investigative Tests

Blood Tests. Blood tests are currently used to check for anemia and other disorders that can produce dementia symptoms. Investigators are researching serum biomarkers, such as the iron transport protein p97, that might help detect the presence of Alzheimer's disease.

Cerebrospinal Fluid Test. Scientists are developing new nanotechnology screening methods that may eventually be used to identify Alzheimer's disease while it is still in its earliest stages and before plaque deposits accumulate. In 2005, a research team announced it had used a bio-barcode assay to detect tiny amounts of a protein called amyloid-beta-derived diffusable ligand (ADDL) in cerebrospinal fluid. ADDLs may be involved in cognitive decline and are a potential biomarker for early stage Alzheimer's disease. Tests for other proteins are also being developed.

Odor Test. Investigators are also using the impairment of smell in Alzheimer's disease to develop tests that require patients to distinguish between odors.

Determining Severity After a Diagnosis Has Been Made

Once a diagnosis has been made, some experts observe that certain factors at the time of diagnosis indicate a higher risk for a more rapid decline:

- Older age
- Being male
- The presence of high blood pressure
- Signs of loss of motor control and coordination
- Tremor
- Social withdrawal
- Loss of appetite and severe weight loss
- Accompanying sensory problems, such as hearing loss and a decline in reading ability
- General physical debility

Developing Drug Treatments for Alzheimer's Disease

Catharine Paddock

Pharmaceutical companies are searching for new preventative and therapeutic drugs to combat Alzheimer's disease. As of 2007 the only classes of Alzheimer's drugs approved for use in humans managed mild to moderate symptoms. In the following selection, Catharine Paddock reports on research presented at the 2007 Alzheimer's Association International Conference on Prevention of Dementia in Washington, D.C., including the status of four possible new Alzheimer's drugs and vaccines. Paddock is a science writer and frequent contributor to *Medical News Today*.

Results from a series of trials on four drugs to treat Alzheimer's appear to bring a new era of hope to patients with the disease, according to scientists reporting their findings to the 2nd Alzheimer's Association International Conference on Prevention of Dementia in Washington, DC [on June 11, 2007]. The confer-

SOURCE: Catharine Paddock, "Four Alzheimer's Drug Trials Bring New Era of Hope," www.medicalnewstoday.com, June 12, 2007. Reproduced by permission.

ence brings together over 1,000 dementia experts from around the world.

The four drugs are an anti-amyloid (Alzhemed), an inhibitor of brain cell death (Dimebon), an "Alzheimer's vaccine" (Immunotherapy Treatment AN1792), and a drug normally used to treat diabetes (Avandia).

Alzheimer's disease is thought to be caused by buildup of a protein called amyloid beta which forms plaques and tangles in the brain, kills off brain cells and interferes with neuron-to-neuron signalling.

Approved treatments for Alzheimer's currently only relieve symptoms for a couple of years and make little impact on the amyloid beta buildup and the progress of the disease. Vice president for Medical and Scientific Relations at the Alzheimer's Association, Dr William Thies said that: "Amyloid as a cause for Alzheimer's and a primary target for therapies and preventions must be thoroughly tested. . . . We need an answer to this question so that we can then sharpen our focus on attacking amyloid and creating better treatments, or change the focus to other areas if the theory is wrong." . . .

> **FAST FACT**
>
> A treatment that delays the onset of Alzheimer's disease (AD), if found, could reduce the number of people diagnosed with AD by 50 percent after 50 years.

Dr Sam Gandy, chair of the Alzheimer's Association's Medical and Scientific Advisory Council said they were very pleased to see so many drugs make it to clinical trials, and was optimistic that: "The odds are quite good that we'll have more effective new treatments for Alzheimer's in the near future."

Developing a new drug is a lengthy and expensive process that takes up to 15 years and on average costs 800 million US dollars. According to the Alzheimer's Association, only 5 out of 10,000 compounds investigated make it to clinical trials, and of those, only one makes it through to approval for treatment. And, in the case of Alzheimer's, there are added challenges; for example, the only definitive diagnosis at the moment involves sampling brain tissue.

Anti-Amyloid: Alzhemed

Tramiprosate, brand name Alzhemed (made by Neurochem) is an orally-administered amyloid beta antagonist that is currently in Phase III clinical trials to assess its safety, efficacy and disease-modifying effects in patients with mild to moderate Alzheimer's.

Alzhemed binds to amyloid beta protein and interferes with its ability to build plaque and poison brain cells.

Dr Paul Aisen, Professor of Neurology and Medicine, and Director of the Memory Disorders Program at the Georgetown University Medical Center, Washington DC, and lead author presented the conference with an update of the trial. The key points were:

- The randomized, double-blind, placebo controlled trial enrolled 1,052 patients from several medical centres in the US and Canada.

- All patients were taking doses of acetylcholinesterase inhibitors, with or without memantine.

- Patients took either the active drug or a placebo twice a day for 18 months and were assessed every three months.

- Assessments included tests of cognitive function, disability, clinical efficacy, and volumetric MRI to assess effect of the disease on brain volume.

Unfortunately Aisen was unable to present any conclusions because there is a lot of complex data that is still being processed. Apparently there are significant unexpected differences in the data coming from the various sites and these need to be accounted for before the results can be finalized.

Gandy said that while the results of the Alzhemed Phase III clinical trial were not available, there was a positive note: "We have learned important lessons about

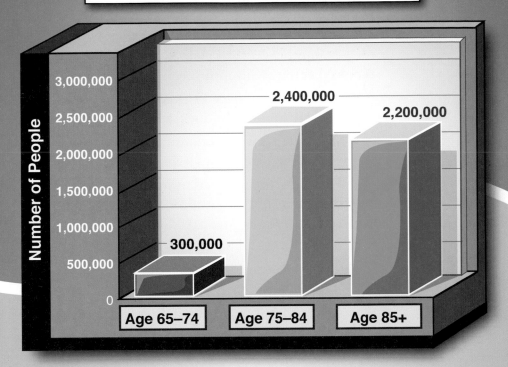

U.S. Incidence of Alzheimer's Disease by Age Group

Number of People

3,000,000
2,500,000
2,000,000
1,500,000
1,000,000
500,000
0

2,400,000

2,200,000

300,000

Age 65–74   Age 75–84   Age 85+

Taken from: "Alzheimer's Disease Facts and Figures," Alzheimer's Association, 2007.
www.alz.org/national/documents/report–2007FactsAndFigures.pdf.

how to do these types of very complex, long-term, large-scale Alzheimer's trials, which in itself is very important because there are now so many promising Alzheimer's therapies in the pipeline," he explained.

Brain Cell Death Inhibitor: Dimebon

Dimebon (made by Medivation) is an orally-administered drug that has shown ability to stop brain cell death in pre-clinical testing for Alzheimer's and Huntington's.

Dimebon appears to offer brain cells protection from amyloid buildup by blocking something that targets their mitochondria. Mitochondria supply cells with energy and are also involved in programmed cell death (apoptosis) which is associated with neurodegenerative diseases like Alzheimer's and ageing.

Dr Rachel Doody, Effie Marie Cain Chair in Alzheimer's Disease Research and Professor of Neurology at Baylor College of Medicine, Houston, Texas reported the 12-month results of a small trial, which was already reported at the six-month stage:

- The trial took place in Russia and enrolled 183 patients with mild to moderated Alzheimer's.
- The patients were randomized to receive Dimebon or placebo three times a day for six months.
- They were then offered to continue in a double blind trial extension for another six months.
- No other anti-dementia medication was allowed.
- Assessments included a battery of cognitive and other tests of behaviour and daily functioning... performed at baseline and then roughly every 3 months.
- The results showed that patients improved significantly compared to baseline on all measures and the drug was well tolerated.

According to Dr William Thies, vice president of medical and scientific affairs at the Alzheimer's Association, Dimebon limits symptoms in a similar way to . . . Aricept [an already approved drug used to treat AD].

Adverse events included dry mouth and sweating and over 30 per cent of the patients dropped out of the trial. This high drop out rate could raise some concerns, said some critics, although the results are promising.

Medivation will be seeking approval for Dimebon in 2010.

"Alzheimer's Vaccine": Immunotherapy Treatment AN1792

AN1792 is a synthetic form of the amyloid beta protein (made by Elan and Wyeth) which was used in an immunotherapeutic clinical trial that was stopped because 6 per cent of the patients began to suffer from inflammation of the brain (encephalitis). However, the researchers followed the patients after the trial.

Dr Michael Grundman, Senior Director of Clinical Development in the Alzheimer's Disease Program at Elan Pharmaceuticals presented their findings to the conference. These showed that 4.5 years after immunization with AN1792, patients who had developed antibodies to amyloid beta continued to show detectable levels of antibodies and slower decline in daily living compared with patients treated with placebo. The key points of their findings were:

- 159 patients/caregiver pairs to took part in the follow-up (30 placebo patients and 129 patients on AN1792).
- Of the 129 AN1792 patients, 25 were classed "antibody responders".
- Compared to the placebo group, the anti-body responders showed significant favourable results in: ability to look after themselves and pursue leisure activities; dependency on caregivers; and memory and thinking skills.

The image on the left shows part of the brain of a mouse genetically engineered with Alzheimer's disease. The right side shows a mouse treated with a vaccine to help prevent Alzheimer's. Researchers hope one day to treat or prevent Alzheimer's in humans. **(AP Images)**

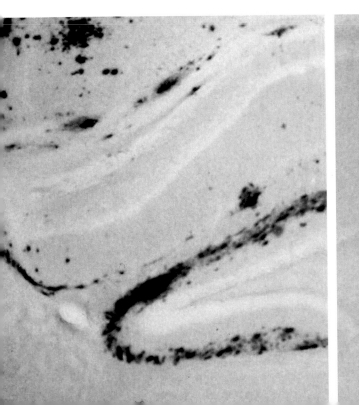

- After the first year, brain volume changes in antibody responders and placebo patients were similar.
- No further cases of encephalitis were observed.

"The favorable results on Activities of Daily Living among the antibody responders in this study support the hypothesis that amyloid beta immunotherapy may have long-term benefits for patients with mild to moderate Alzheimer's and their caregivers," said Grundman.

Diabetes Drug: Avandia

Rosiglitazone, brand name Avandia (made by Glaxo-SmithKline) is already approved for treatment of type 2 diabetes (but not for Alzheimer's). It lowers blood sugar by helping cells use insulin more effectively.

Scientists have speculated that Avandia may also be able to help Alzheimer's patients because of its effect on brain inflammation and other processes associated with neurodegenerative diseases.

However, in recent months, Avandia has been in the spotlight because a recent study that reviewed the available published research suggested that diabetes patients on Avandia were at increased risk of heart attack and death from cardiovascular causes.

Researchers studied the effect of an extended release form of Avandia (Rosiglitazone XR) on Alzheimer's patients for 12 months. This was a follow-up open-label extension to a randomized controlled trial.

The results suggested that Avandia may help some Alzheimer's patients depending on their genetic make up. Patients that were "APOE e4 negative" did benefit from the treatment, they showed some improvement. But patients who were "APOE e4 positive" either did not improve or continued to decline. [APOE e4 is a form of a gene linked to Alzheimer's.] The key points of the study were:

- 337 patients with mild to moderate Alzheimer's enrolled in the study and 82 per cent of them completed it.

- 7 per cent pulled out because of adverse events.

- 48 per cent had one or more adverse events (mostly peripheral oedema, or fluid accumulation, in the legs or sacral region, nasopharyngitis, or inflammation of the nasal passages and pharynx).

- 9 per cent had one or more severe adverse events, each of which occurred in 1 per cent or less of the patients (except for fractures, 2 per cent).

- Few patients had clinically significant changes in heart rate (less than 1 per cent) or abnormal ECG [electrocardiogram] readings (2 per cent).

- Insulin and glycemic control measures were within the range expected for older people with low insulin resistance.

Although there is controversy surrounding the use of Avandia as a type 2 diabetes drug because of the link with elevated heart problem risks, these risks could be outweighed by the potential benefits when considering the benefit-risk profile of a person with Alzheimer's.

Global Clinical Vice President, Neurology, at Glaxo-SmithKline, Dr Michael Gold said that Avandia appeared to have a safety profile similar to that already seen in diabetes type 2 patients. He added that "Rosiglitazone XR (Avandia) appeared to be generally well tolerated in subjects with Alzheimer's for up to 72 weeks."

Thies said: "There is value in continuing to study rosiglitazone in Alzheimer's. We need to attack the disease through multiple mechanisms, and the only way we can learn with certainty about issues of safety and efficacy in Alzheimer's is through clinical trials."

"There are risks involved in clinical studies, and we do need to ensure that all risks are thoroughly described and explained to study participants and family members. That's why we have informed consent, and why the process is so important," he added.

Alternative Treatments

Alzheimer's Association

Alternative therapies are growing in popularity in the United States and abroad. However, until recently few scientific studies have tested the efficacy of alternative therapies. Alternative medicine proponents assert that various vitamins, minerals, and foods are beneficial in preventing Alzheimer's disease (AD), combating dementia and other symptoms, slowing the progression of the disease, or aiding the efficacy of traditional medicine. The following article, compiled by the Alzheimer's Association, discusses forms of alternative AD therapies (sometimes called supplemental therapies or complementary medicine), while cautioning that researchers disagree on their ultimate usefulness and safety. The Alzheimer's Association is the leading U.S. organization providing information and support for Alzheimer's patients, families, and researchers.

A growing number of herbal remedies, vitamins and other dietary supplements are promoted as memory enhancers or treatments for Alzheimer's disease and related diseases. Claims about the safety and

SOURCE: "Alternative Treatments," Alzheimer's Association (www.alz.org), 2007. Copyright © 2007 Alzheimer's Association, www.alz.org, (800) 272-3900. Reproduced with the permission of the Alzheimer's Association.

effectiveness of these products, however, are based largely on testimonials, tradition and a rather small body of scientific research. The rigorous scientific research required by the U.S. Food and Drug Administration (FDA) for the approval of a prescription drug is not required by law for the marketing of dietary supplements.

Concerns About Alternative Therapies

Although many of these remedies may be valid candidates for treatments, there are legitimate concerns about using these drugs as an alternative or in addition to physician-prescribed therapy:

- **Effectiveness and safety are unknown.** The maker of a dietary supplement is not required to provide the FDA with the evidence on which it bases its claims for safety and effectiveness.
- **Purity is unknown.** The FDA has no authority over supplement production. It is a manufacturer's responsibility to develop and enforce its own guidelines for ensuring that its products are safe and contain the ingredients listed on the label in the specified amounts.
- **Bad reactions are not routinely monitored.** Manufacturers are not required to report to the FDA any problems that consumers experience after taking their products. The agency does provide voluntary reporting channels for manufacturers, health care professionals, and consumers, and will issue warnings about product when there is cause for concern.
- **Dietary supplements can have serious interactions with prescribed medications.** No supplement should be taken without first consulting a physician.

Coenzyme Q10

Coenzyme Q10, or ubiquinone, is an antioxidant that occurs naturally in the body and is needed for normal cell reactions. This compound has not been studied for its effectiveness in treating Alzheimer's.

A synthetic version of this compound, called idebenone, was tested for Alzheimer's disease but did not show favorable results. Little is known about what dosage of coenzyme Q10 is considered safe, and there could be harmful effects if too much is taken.

Coral Calcium

"Coral" calcium supplements have been heavily marketed as a cure for Alzheimer's disease, cancer and other serious illnesses. Coral calcium is a form of calcium carbonate claimed to be derived from the shells of formerly living organisms that once made up coral reefs.

In June 2003, the Federal Trade Commission (FTC) and the Food and Drug Administration (FDA) filed a formal complaint against the promoters and distributors of coral calcium. The agencies state that they are aware of no competent and reliable scientific evidence supporting the exaggerated health claims and that such unsupported claims are unlawful.

Coral calcium differs from ordinary calcium supplements only in that it contains traces of some additional minerals incorporated into the shells by the metabolic processes of the animals that formed them. It offers no extraordinary health benefits. Most experts recommend that individuals who need to take a calcium supplement for bone health take a purified preparation marketed by a reputable manufacturer.

Ginkgo Biloba

Ginkgo biloba is a plant extract containing several compounds that may have positive effects on cells within the brain and the body. *Ginkgo biloba* is thought to have both antioxidant and anti-inflammatory properties, to protect cell membranes and to regulate neurotransmitter function. *Ginkgo* has been used for centuries in traditional

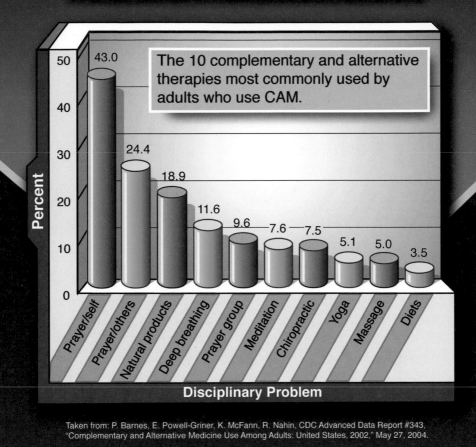

Ten Most Common Alternative Medicine (CAM) Therapies—2002

The 10 complementary and alternative therapies most commonly used by adults who use CAM.

Percent

- Prayer/self: 43.0
- Prayer/others: 24.4
- Natural products: 18.9
- Deep breathing: 11.6
- Prayer group: 9.6
- Meditation: 7.6
- Chiropractic: 7.5
- Yoga: 5.1
- Massage: 5.0
- Diets: 3.5

Disciplinary Problem

Taken from: P. Barnes, E. Powell-Griner, K. McFann, R. Nahin, CDC Advanced Data Report #343, "Complementary and Alternative Medicine Use Among Adults: United States, 2002," May 27, 2004.

Chinese medicine and currently is being used in Europe to alleviate cognitive symptoms associated with a number of neurological conditions.

In a study published in the *Journal of the American Medical Association*, Pierre L. Le Bars, M.D., Ph.D., of the New York Institute for Medical Research, and his colleagues observed in some participants a modest improvement in cognition, activities of daily living (such as eating and dressing) and social behavior. The researchers found no measurable difference in overall impairment.

Results from this study show that *Ginkgo* may help some individuals with Alzheimer's disease, but further research is needed to determine the exact mechanisms by which *Ginkgo* works in the body. Also, results from this study are considered preliminary because of the low number of participants, about 200 people.

Few side effects are associated with the use of *Ginkgo*, but it is known to reduce the ability of blood to clot, potentially leading to more serious conditions, such as internal bleeding. This risk may increase if *Ginkgo biloba* is taken in combination with other blood-thinning drugs, such as aspirin and warfarin.

Currently, a large federally funded multicenter trial with about 3,000 participants is investigating whether *Ginkgo* may help prevent or delay the onset of Alzheimer's disease or vascular dementia.

Huperzine A

Huperzine A (pronounced *HOOP-ur-zeen*) is a moss extract that has been used in traditional Chinese medicine for centuries. It has properties similar to those of cholinesterase inhibitors, one class of FDA-approved Alzheimer medications. As a result, it is promoted as a treatment for Alzheimer's disease.

Evidence from small studies shows that the effectiveness of huperzine A may be comparable to that of the approved drugs. In Spring 2004, the National Institute on Aging (NIA) launched the first large U.S. clinical trial of huperzine A as a treatment for mild to moderate Alzheimer's disease.

Because currently available formulations of huperzine A are dietary supplements, they are unregulated and manufactured with no uniform standards. If used in combination with FDA-approved Alzheimer drugs, an individual could increase the risks of serious side effects.

Omega-3 Fatty Acids

Omega-3s are a type of polyunsaturated fatty acid (PUFA). Research has linked certain types of omega-3s to a reduced risk of heart disease and stroke.

The U.S. Food and Drug Administration (FDA) permits supplements and foods to display labels with "a qualified health claim" for two omega-3s called docosahexaneoic acid (DHA) and eicosapentaenoic acid (EPA). The labels may state, "Supportive but not conclusive research shows that consumption of EPA and DHA omega-3 fatty acids may reduce the risk of coronary heart disease," and then list the amount of DHA or EPA in the product. The FDA recommends taking no more than a combined total of 3 grams of DHA or EPA a day, with no more than 2 grams from supplements.

Research has also linked high intake of omega-3s to a possible reduction in risk of dementia or cognitive decline. The chief omega-3 in the brain is DHA, which is found in the fatty membranes that surround nerve cells, especially at the microscopic junctions where cells connect to one another.

A Jan. 25, 2006, literature review by the Cochrane Collaboration found that published research does not currently include any clinical trials large enough to recommend omega-3 supplements to prevent cognitive decline or dementia. But the reviewers found enough laboratory and epidemiological studies to conclude this should be a priority area for further research.

According to the review, results of at least two larger clinical trials are expected in 2008. The Cochrane Collaboration is an independent, nonprofit organization that makes objective assessments of available evidence on a variety of issues in treatment and health care.

Theories about why omega-3s might influence dementia risk include their benefit for the heart and blood vessels; anti-inflammatory effects; and support and protection of nerve cell membranes. There is also preliminary evidence that omega-3s may also be of some benefit in depression and bipolar disorder (manic depression).

FAST FACT

According to a study by the Centers for Disease Control (CDC), 74.1 percent of U.S. adults have used some form of alternative medicine, excluding daily multivitamins.

A report in the April 2006 *Nature* described the first direct evidence for how omega-3s might have a helpful effect on nerve cells (neurons). Working with laboratory cell cultures, the researchers found that omega-3s stimulate growth of the branches that connect one cell to another. Rich branching creates a dense "neuron forest," which provides the basis of the brain's capacity to process, store and retrieve information.

Phosphatidylserine

Phosphatidylserine (pronounced *FOS-fuh-TIE-dil-sair-een*) is a kind of lipid, or fat, that is the primary component of the membranes that surround nerve cells. In

A growing number of herbal remedies, vitamins, and other supplements are promoted as memory enhancers or treatments for Alzheimer's disease. Most of these claims are unproven.
(Will & Deni McIntyre / Photo Researchers, Inc.)

Alzheimer's disease and similar disorders, nerve cells degenerate for reasons that are not yet understood. The theory behind treatment with phosphatidylserine is its use may shore up the cell membrane and possibly protect cells from degenerating.

The first clinical trials with phosphatidylserine were conducted with a form derived from the brain cells of cows. Some of these trials had promising results. However, most trials were with small samples of participants.

This line of investigation came to an end in the 1990s over concerns about mad cow disease. There have been some animal studies since then to see whether phosphatidylserine derived from soy may be a potential treatment. A report was published in 2000 about a clinical trial with 18 participants with age-associated memory impairment who were treated with phosphatidylserine. The authors concluded that the results were encouraging but that there would need to be large carefully controlled trials to determine if this could be a viable treatment.

CHAPTER 2

Alzheimer's Issues and Controversies

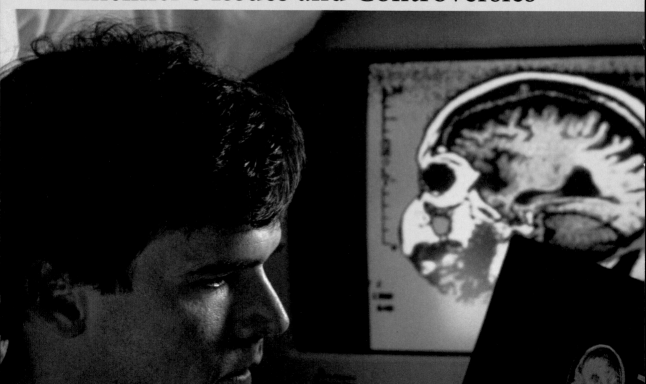

Embryonic Stem Cell Research Is Needed for Alzheimer's Disease

Lawrence S. Goldstein

Human embryonic stem cell research is a controversial social issue. Proponents, including many scientists, assert that embryonic stem cell research is a vital developing field that promises significant breakthroughs on some of the most complex and least understood diseases and disorders. Alzheimer's researcher Lawrence S. Goldstein gave the following testimony to the U.S. Senate in support of embryonic stem cell research and expanded federal government investment in stem-cell-based Alzheimer's research. Goldstein is a professor of cellular and molecular medicine at the University of California at San Diego. He helped establish the San Diego Consortium for Regenerative Medicine and is currently director of the University of California at San Diego Stem Cell Program.

M y research that is relevant to today's hearing is focused on understanding the molecular mechanisms that are used to move vital material inside neurons, brain cells. And we study and are

Photo on facing page. Research into the causes and possible cures of Alzheimer's disease is ongoing. (Will & Deni McIntyre/Photo Researchers, Inc.)

SOURCE: Lawrence S. Goldstein, Ph.D., "Testimony to U.S. Senate Special Committee on Aging 'Exploring the Promise of Embryonic Stem Cell Research'," The Federal News Service, June 8, 2005. Copyright © 2005 The Federal News Service, Inc. Reproduced by permission.

trying to learn how failures of those movements contribute to the development of diseases such as Alzheimer's disease, Huntington's disease, Parkinson's disease and perhaps others, including mad cow disease.

Now, before I tell you about my science I do want to just take a moment and thank you, Senator [Gordon H.] Smith and your colleagues there, for your long standing support of the federal investment in biomedical research and in particular for your leadership in developing federal funding, we hope, for broader areas of human embryonic stem cell research. I respect your courage on this issue, I know it's not easy. With respect to the science I want to discuss how my research is trying to take advantage of the enormous scientific and medical opportunity provided by human embryonic stem cells. I do want to be cautious. I want to stress that scientific progress in the fight against these diseases, particularly Alzheimer's disease, is very difficult.

This is a hard problem and sometimes our advances are agonizingly slow, even when we have the best tools available to us. And importantly, it's very hard to guarantee the rate at which we can progress. Nonetheless, I and many of my colleagues think that human embryonic stem cells potentially hold the key to major advances in the search for new understanding of and new treatments for these terrible diseases.

Embryonic Stem Cells Provide New Research Opportunities

Now, for many diseases, including for example juvenile diabetes as [former NBA player Chris] Dudley just testified about, there is great enthusiasm for using human embryonic stem cells to replace cells that are lost in disease.

For Alzheimer's disease, however, I think that there may be an even more powerful approach to the use of human embryonic stem cells to develop new understanding and new therapies.

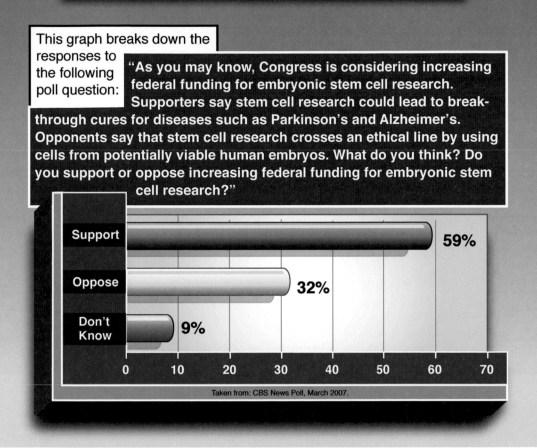

U.S. Support for Legislation Expanding Funding for Stem Cell Research, 2007

This graph breaks down the responses to the following poll question:

"As you may know, Congress is considering increasing federal funding for embryonic stem cell research. Supporters say stem cell research could lead to break-through cures for diseases such as Parkinson's and Alzheimer's. Opponents say that stem cell research crosses an ethical line by using cells from potentially viable human embryos. What do you think? Do you support or oppose increasing federal funding for embryonic stem cell research?"

Response	Percentage
Support	59%
Oppose	32%
Don't Know	9%

Taken from: CBS News Poll, March 2007.

And that's what I want to talk about today, is another way of taking advantage of this enormous scientific opportunity. Now, before doing that I need to explain why it is so hard to learn what happens, what goes wrong in brain cells in brain diseases such as Alzheimer's disease.

And the bottom line, in a sense, and an important basic principle is that you can rarely, if ever, do the kinds of biochemical and cellular experiments on brain cells of human patients while they're still alive and while they're still in the earliest and, we hope, treatable stages of the disease.

I think you can understand why a patient might not be willing to give their brain to experiments before they died of the disorder, they still need their brain, after all. So much of what we learn and can learn about the basic cell biology and biochemistry of brain cells that have this disease comes from studying brain cells from people who've died of the disease already and hence were in late stages.

And the problem is that we then end up studying the cells and the brain after most of the damage has already happened. And if you think about it, this is in some ways like trying to detect and prevent or learning to detect and prevent plane crashes by studying the pattern of wreckage on the ground after planes have already crashed. There's a great deal that's missing.

Understanding the Earliest Stages of Alzheimer's Disease

What we really need in a sense is the black box. We need the black box to reveal what went wrong in the earliest stages of the disease, the nature of the cellular changes and malfunctions so that we can then learn to treat or prevent these diseases. And so in our search for understanding of Alzheimer's disease we're effectively looking for the black box of this disorder.

The question then is how to find that. Because after all, we need to learn what those early changes are so that we might learn to fix them. Now, a very important approach that we've used for the past decade in the fight against Alzheimer's disease is to take advantage of the existence of very rare forms of the disease that are caused by large genetic changes that give rise to what we call hereditary Alzheimer's disease.

And these large genetic changes are in many cases known. And so what we can do is we can take these large genetic changes and we can introduce them into laboratory animals such as mice. And we can then study the brain cells from these mice and learn what cellular changes and what changes in the brain happen in these mice that have these large scale genetic changes that cause Alzheimer's disease in people.

Stem Cells Help Researchers Study Genetic Changes in Brain Cells

The problem is that while we've learned a great deal from this approach, and indeed there are many ideas that my lab and others have generated from this approach, I'm sure you realize that people are not just big mice. And there are many important differences in the physiology of our cells and our brains that lead us to need to test ideas that come from studying mice in human people, human patients, and in particular if we're going to develop treatments and drugs.

And, of course, the question then is how to do that, and that's where human embryonic stem cells provide what I think is going to be an incredibly important tool for doing this. And this is what we're trying to do now in my laboratory. What we're trying to do is to learn to take these human embryonic stem cells and invert them into the brain cells, the types of brain cells that die and fail to function properly in the earliest stages of Alzheimer's disease.

And some of the properties of these cells make it possible for us to make the genetic changes, the large genetic changes in these cells that cause hereditary Alzheimer's disease in people. And so what we can then do with these brain cells in a dish that have Alzheimer's disease because of the genetic changes, is to study them at their earliest stages and test our ideas that come from studying mice.

And ultimately we think as we learn which ideas are truly correct, which I hope we'll do in the next few years, we can use these cells, we believe, to begin testing and developing new drugs that we can use to treat this terrible disorder. Because as you know we have very little in the way of drugs to treat Alzheimer's disease.

> **FAST FACT**
>
> The National Institutes of Health estimate that 100 million Americans suffer from over seventy different diseases and injuries that could potentially benefit from embryonic stem cell research.

Human embryonic stem cell research is seen by some scientists as a vital developing field that promises significant breakthroughs with diseases such as Alzheimer's. (AP Images)

Embryonic Stem Cells May Help Determine Who Is at Risk

Now, there's a second problem in treating and understanding diseases such as Alzheimer's disease where human embryonic stem cells also have a major contribution to potentially make. And that comes from the observation that most Alzheimer's disease is what we call sporadic.

It is not caused by large genetic changes that are strictly hereditary. Instead it appears to occur almost randomly. However, there is a great deal of evidence that suggests that each one of us has different genetic susceptibility or potential genetic resistance to the development of this disorder.

And we think that there are many small genetic changes that each of us harbors in different combinations that interact together or interact with the environment to cause us to either develop or not develop this disease. And the problem is that we don't have a way to study this major form of the disease in animals.

It's a huge limitation. These embryonic stem cells, however, potentially give us a way to crack that problem, because each different embryonic stem cell line has different combinations of these small genetic changes, and we think that we can convert those cells, these different cell lines, to the brain cells that malfunction in this disease and study how those small genetic changes lead to the different cell behavior cell function in the disease that causes those symptoms.

Many Embryonic Stem Cell Lines Are Needed

And this is where the availability of many different embryonic stem cell lines may turn out to be crucial in the fight against this disorder, because we can begin to evaluate how our different genetic constitutions confer susceptibility or resistance to this disorder and potentially teach us how to predict which people will respond to different types of treatments or for whom a particular drug will not work.

And thus [it will] help us both in the development of clinical trials, the development of drugs and not treating people with drugs that aren't going to help them. But obviously these are very difficult skills. We have to work very hard to get there and we're going to need far more than a single scientist laboring in San Diego to make the kinds of breakthroughs that are going to be needed on this one disorder.

I want to close with just saying that the ideas that I've just described and the approaches that I've just described for Alzheimer's disease will, I believe, be very valuable in the fight against Parkinson's disease, Huntington's disease, Lou Gehrig's disease and other neurodegenerative diseases where we don't even understand them well enough to give them a name.

Embryonic Stem Cell Research Is Unlikely to Benefit Alzheimer's Patients

Rick Weiss

Not only is the practice of using embryonic stem cells controversial, there is also significant debate about which diseases would most benefit from increased funding of embryonic stem cell research. While many opponents object to the use of embryonic stem cells on moral or ethical grounds, Rick Weiss explains in the following viewpoint that others are skeptical of their ultimate utility. Weiss discusses the different criticisms and possible shortcomings of using embryonic stem cells in Alzheimer's research. Weiss is a science and medical reporter for the *Washington Post*.

R onald Reagan's death from Alzheimer's disease Saturday [June 5, 2004] has triggered an outpouring of support for human embryonic stem cell research. Building on comments made by Nancy Reagan last month, scores of senators on Monday called upon

President [George W.] Bush to loosen his restrictions on the controversial research, which requires the destruction of human embryos. Patient groups have also chimed in, and Senate Majority Leader Bill Frist (R-Tenn.) on Tuesday added his support for a policy review. It is the kind of advocacy that researchers have craved for years, and none wants to slow its momentum.

But the infrequently voiced reality, stem cell experts confess, is that, of all the diseases that may someday be cured by embryonic stem cell treatments, Alzheimer's is among the least likely to benefit. "I think the chance of doing repairs to Alzheimer's brains by putting in stem cells is small," said stem cell researcher Michael Shelanski, co-director of the Taub Institute for Research on Alzheimer's Disease and the Aging Brain at the Columbia University Medical Center in New York, echoing many other experts. "I personally think we're going to get other therapies for Alzheimer's a lot sooner."

Stem Cells May Benefit Other Diseases More than Alzheimer's

Stem cell transplants show great potential for other diseases as such as Parkinson's and diabetes, scientists said. Someday, embryo cell studies may lead to insights into Alzheimer's. If nothing else, some said, stem cells bearing the genetic hallmarks of Alzheimer's may help scientists assess the potential usefulness of new drugs.

But given the lack of any serious suggestion that stem cells themselves have practical potential to treat Alzheimer's, the Reagan-inspired tidal wave of enthusiasm stands as an example of how easily a modest line of scientific inquiry can grow in the public mind to mythological proportions.

It is a distortion that some admit is not being aggressively corrected by scientists. "To start with, people need a fairy tale," said Ronald D.G. McKay, a stem cell researcher at the National Institute of Neurological Disorders and

Stroke. "Maybe that's unfair, but they need a story line that's relatively simple to understand."

Human embryonic stem cells have the capacity to morph into virtually any kind of tissue, leading many scientists to believe they could serve as a "universal patch" for injured organs. Some studies have suggested, for example, that stem cells injected into an injured heart can spur the development of healthy new heart muscle.

Among the more promising targets of such "cellular therapies" are: Parkinson's disease, which affects a small and specialized population of brain cells; type-1 diabetes, caused by the loss of discrete insulin-producing cells in the pancreas; and spinal cord injuries in which a few crucial nerve cells die, such as the injury that paralyzed actor Christopher Reeve.

Politicians and Hollywood Personalities Weigh In

In part as a result of her friendship with HollyWood personalities Doug Wick, Lucy Fisher, and Jerry and Janet Zucker—all of whom have become stem cell activists because they have children with diabetes—Nancy Reagan became interested in stem cells and their off-cited, if largely theoretical, potential for treating Alzheimer's. Over the years, she has become more vocal on the issue.

On May 8, with her husband's brain ravaged by Alzheimer's disease, Nancy Reagan addressed a biomedical research fundraiser in Los Angeles and spoke out forcefully.

"I just don't see how we can turn our backs on this," she said, in an oblique cut at Bush, who placed tight limits on the field in August 2001 to protect, he said, the earliest stages of life.

Since Reagan's death, many others have joined the call to enlist embryonic stem cells in the war on Alzheimer's, including some new converts. Among the 58 senators who signed the letter to Bush were 14 Republicans and several abortion opponents—evidence that the Reagan connec-

Ronald Reagan, 40th president of the United States, was diagnosed with Alzheimer's in 1994. His death from the disease in 2004 triggered an outpouring of support for human embryonic stem cell research. (**Library of Congress**)

tion is providing "political cover," said Sean Tipton of the Coalition for the Advancement of Medical Research, a stem cell advocacy group.

Alzheimer's Research Is More Complicated

But in contrast to Parkinson's, diabetes and spinal injuries, Alzheimer's disease involves the loss of huge numbers and varieties of the brain's 100 billion nerve cells—and countless connections, or synapses, among them. "The complex architecture of the brain, the fact that it's

U.S. Support for Embryonic Stem Cell Research

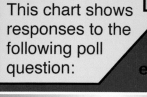

This chart shows responses to the following poll question: "Do you support or oppose embryonic stem cell research?"

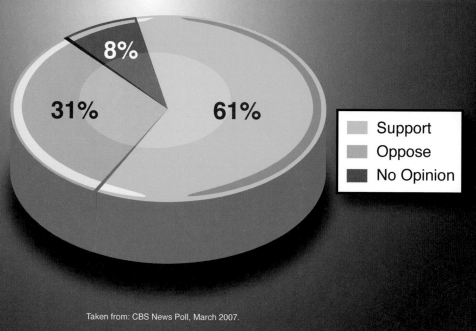

8%

31%

61%

Support
Oppose
No Opinion

Taken from: CBS News Poll, March 2007.

a diffuse disease with neuronal loss in numerous places and with synaptic loss, all this is a problem" for any strategy involving cell replacement, said Huntington Potter, a brain researcher at the University of South Florida in Tampa and chief executive of the Johnnie B. Byrd Institute for Alzheimer's Research.

"We don't even know what are the best cells to replace initially," added Lawrence S.B. Goldstein, who studies stem cells and Alzheimer's disease at the University of California at San Diego. "It's complicated."

Political Challenges to Embryonic Stem Cell Research

Goldstein and others emphasized the future Alzheimer's patients could benefit if stem cell research is allowed to blossom. Scientists suspect, for example, that stem cell studies could help identify the molecular errors that underlie Alzheimer's, which in turn would help chemists design drugs to slow or even reverse the disease.

But that line of work could face formidable political hurdles. That is because the most frequently cited approach would require not just stem cells from spare embryos donated by fertility clinics—a currently untapped source of cells that many want Bush to make available to federally funded researchers. It would also require the creation of cloned human embryos made from cells taken from Alzheimer's patients. From such embryos, stem cells bearing the still-unidentified defects underlying Alzheimer's could be removed and coaxed to grow into brain cells in lab dishes, and their development could be compared to the development of normal brain cells.

While that experiment could shed important light on the earliest—and perhaps most treatable—stages of Alzheimer's, a majority in Congress have said that the creation of cloned human embryos is an ethical line they are unwilling to cross.

Less controversial uses of stem cells may also lead to insights, Goldstein and others said. The key, said Harvard stem cell researcher George Daley, is not to get "preoccupied with stem cells as cellular therapies." Their real value for Alzheimer's will be as laboratory tools to explore basic questions of biology, Daley said.

Unfortunately, said James Battey, who directs stem cell research for the National Institutes of Health, "that

FAST FACT

In 2001 President George W. Bush restricted federal money to embryonic stem cell lines that already existed, estimated to be about seventy-eight at that time. The number of viable stem cell lines available as of 2004 was thought to be only twenty-two.

is not necessarily the way I hear the disease community talking. They tend to focus on the immediate use of stem cells for their disease or disorder."

It is not clear whether the recent wave of stem cell support will persist as it becomes clearer that cures remain far off—and, in the case of Alzheimer's, unlikely. Basic research with stem cells is just as deserving of support as therapeutic trials, Battey said, "but it's a much harder sell."

"The public should understand that science is not like making widgets," he said. "We're exploring the unknown, and by definition we don't know where it's going to take us."

Alzheimer's Research Is Too Narrowly Focused on One Dominant Hypothesis

Sharon Begley

Sharon Begley, a staff reporter for the *Wall Street Journal*, asserts that the field of Alzheimer's research is dominated by one significant hypothesis about the causes of Alzheimer's disease. She claims that alternative theories receive less attention from scientific journals, less attention from the scientific community, and less research funding, perhaps excluding new and possibly groundbreaking research on Alzheimer's disease.

Jie Shen describes the past two years of her scientific life as "torture," but she can't say she wasn't warned. In the mid-1990s, as a young researcher in the lab of a Nobel-winning neuroscientist, she grew curious about alternatives to the leading hypothesis of Alzheimer's disease, and in virtually any other field she would have been free, even encouraged, to follow her scientific curiosity wherever it led. But her mentor warned her off. Alzheimer's, he said, is not like other fields.

SOURCE: Sharon Begley, "Is Alzheimer's Field Blocking Research Into Other Causes?" *Wall Street Journal,* April 9, 2004. Republished with permission of *Wall Street Journal,* conveyed through Copyright Clearance Center, Inc.

She found that out the hard way during an odyssey that has finally culminated in the publication of an eye-opening paper. In a nutshell, a team led by Dr. Shen, a molecular geneticist and neurobiologist at Harvard Medical School, Boston, shut down two mouse genes whose human forms have been linked to inherited forms of Alzheimer's.

According to the leading theory of the disease, these so-called presenilin genes are involved in the production of beta-amyloid, a protein that forms gumball-like "plaques" in the brain. Those plaques, in turn, are widely thought to kill brain cells, erase synapses and memory, and lead, ultimately and often blessedly, to death.

But adult mice missing the presenilin genes, and hence the supposedly toxic amyloid protein, still suffered memory problems and brain-cell death, just as in Alzheimer's. Dr. Shen and her colleagues concluded that amyloid is something the brain likely needs in order to think, remember and keep neurons alive, not something that gums it up, as the "amyloid hypothesis" holds.

FAST FACT

An estimated $3.5 billion has been spent on Alzheimer's research in the United States since the late 1970s. In contrast, the U.S. government spent $2.6 billion on domestic and global HIV/AIDS research in 2002 alone.

Difficulties Getting New Theories Published

When the Harvard scientists submitted their findings to two leading journals beginning in 2002, they hit a brick wall. One peer-reviewer shot back with a long list of criticisms that took them months to address. Another demanded they figure out the molecular mechanism behind the effects in the mice, and then when they did that, demanded yet more detail—the mechanism underlying the mechanism, as it were—something pretty much unheard of for a paper of this kind.

"Powerful people in this field think that amyloid causes Alzheimer's and won't consider research that questions the amyloid hypothesis," says one of the Harvard scientists. Competing theories blame other proteins (including those called APP [amyloid precursor protein] and tau), toxic metals, cholesterol or inflammation for Alzheimer's.

NIH Funding for Research on Various Diseases

This table displays funding levels for various diseases, conditions, and research areas.

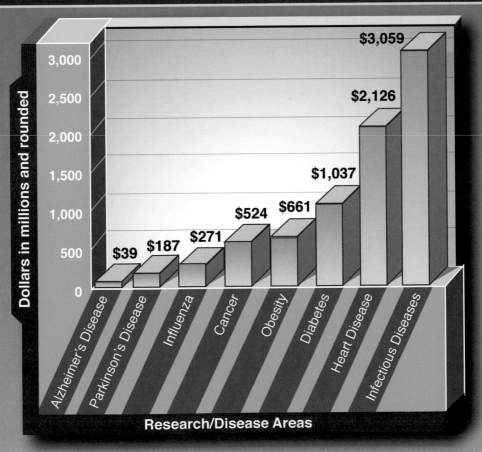

Taken from: National Institutes of Health, "Estimates of Funding for Various Diseases," 2008. www.nih.gov/news/fundingresearchareas.htm.

The Harvard team thinks it would have been nice for the world to know its results two years ago, not yesterday when they were finally published in the journal *Neuron*. "One day," says one of the *Neuron* authors, "I'll write a book, 'The Dark Side of Science.'"

Amyloid enthusiasts deny that they have formed some kind of cabal. They believe that amyloid offers the best shot at defeating Alzheimer's and so view the pursuit of other avenues as a waste of resources. But something else seems to be at work.

"Whenever you have a field with limited funding, and a small number of people with big egos who have everything invested in one idea, you have the right chemistry for one theory to become so pervasive nothing else can flourish," says Zaven Khachaturian, who ran research at the National Institute of Aging from 1977 to 1995. He calls the dominance of the amyloid hypothesis and the strangling of alternatives "one of the most important issues in science today."

One Hypothesis Rules Alzheimer's Research

The result of the amyloid orthodoxy is that for 20 years this one hypothesis has ruled Alzheimer's, dominating the research of scientists seeking understanding and pharmaceutical companies seeking treatments. "The amyloid people are very powerful, and have been dogmatic in opposing alternative [hypotheses]," says molecular biologist Rachael Neve of Harvard.

Despite hundreds of experiments casting doubt on the neurotoxicity of amyloid, maverick and innovative ideas get crushed. As my colleague Bernard Wysocki reported in December [2003], after Ashley Bush of Harvard broke with the amyloid camp, journals rejected his papers and funding agencies turned down his grant proposals.

"It has been very difficult to get funding for anything that's not based on the amyloid cascade, or to publish al-

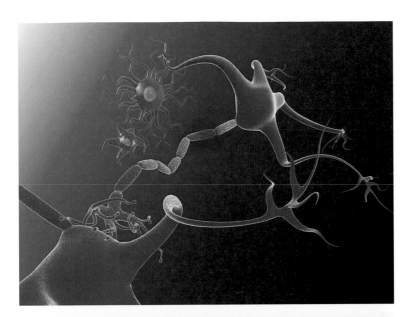

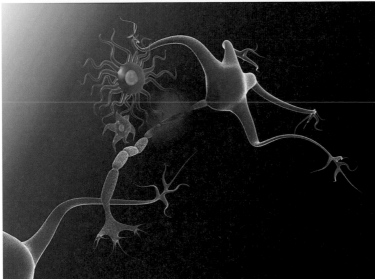

Computer artwork of the early and late stages of Alzheimer's disease in nerve cells in the brain. Protein plaques (brown areas) formed in the brain are thought to kill brain cells. (Gunilla Elam/ Photo Researchers, Inc.)

ternatives to the amyloid hypothesis in top-tier journals," says Thomas Wisniewski, associate professor of neurology and pathology at New York University School of Medicine in New York City.

Such dogmatism is usually a bad idea in science, and when it comes to Alzheimer's, the effect has been nothing short of tragic. By putting almost all its eggs in the amyloid basket, the Alzheimer's establishment has impeded progress on the disease. Because research chasing the demon amyloid gets the lion's share of financial support and dominates the high-profile journals, antiamyloid treatments receive most of the R&D support, too. Few other approaches to cures are in the pipeline.

"I think we've lost some time," says Dr. Wisniewski. Neuropathologist George Perry of Case Western Reserve University, Cleveland, draws an analogy to the criminal-justice system. "Executing beta-amyloid," he says, "leaves the killer loose in the brain."

The Alzheimer's Field Supports Many Lines of Research

Gabrielle Strobel and Martin Citron

In the following interview conducted by Gabrielle Strobel, researcher Martin Citron discusses how the field of Alzheimer's research is open to many divergent theories on the causes of Alzheimer's disease. Citron dismisses the criticism that Alzheimer's disease research is too narrowly focused on a single, dominant hypothesis. He notes that several promising lines of research are currently being pursued. Citron is the associate director of research at Amgen, an international biotechnology company. Strobel conducted this interview with Citron for the Alzheimer's Research Forum, an online portal for Alzheimer's research information.

G*abrielle Strobel: The Holy Grail in AD [Alzheimer's disease] diagnostics right now is finding a robust, predictive marker for presymptomatic AD. This will be even more important once experimental treatments look like they might work. What, to you, are the most promising leads?*

SOURCE: Gabrielle Strobel and Martin Citron, "The Forum Interviews: Martin Citron," Alzheimer's Research Forum, July 9, 2004. Reprinted with permission from the Alzheimer Research Forum.

Martin Citron: The brain imaging field, particularly amyloid [a protein that forms "plaques" in the brain; many scientists think amyloid causes the symptoms of Alzheimer's] imaging and brain volume measurements at this point. I haven't come across anything in terms of straightforward serum markers other than those things that have been in discussion for many years, each of which has problems.

I want to ask you a general question about AD research. In April [2004] two columns by Sharon Begley in the Wall Street Journal *brought into public view what some scientists in the field have been saying for years. She charged that*

Alzheimer's Research Centers Across the United States

The National Institute on Aging funds Alzheimer's Disease Centers (ADCs) at major medical institutions across the United States.

the amyloid hypothesis has monopolized AD research to the exclusion of all other approaches. She writes that this slows down progress, has put all therapeutic eggs in one basket, and that the amyloid hypothesis is wrong, to boot. Have you read this?

Yes.

What's your view?

I personally think the columns misrepresent the big picture. They remind me a bit of the controversy on whether HIV is the cause of AIDS or not. I recall in the early days, when there were no HIV drugs, this discussion was very active. There were people who had quite some arguments against the hypothesis that HIV causes AIDS, for example the fact that you couldn't detect significant amounts of the virus in the blood. While all these people were articulate and vociferous about the shortcomings of the HIV hypothesis, they didn't come up with fully testable alternative hypotheses, and now that the drugs are known to work the issue has died down. Everybody in our field knows the shortcomings of the amyloid hypothesis. I find that these two articles in the *Wall Street Journal* miss the point on several angles.

Which ones?

For example, it cites the work of Ashley Bush and the clioquinol [a pharmaceutical drug] trial as an example of something that's outside the amyloid field. But if one reads his papers, one of the major assumptions is that clioquinol reduces amyloid, so I think his work takes a special angle on the amyloid field but is within it. The other story was Jie Shen's presenilin mutations as loss of function. Jie knocked out all four presenilin alleles—PS1, PS2—and gets a dramatic phenotype. In the Alzheimer's brain, you may have partial loss of function of one of the presenilin alleles plus you have the other three present, too. Now, does her mouse totally model what's happening in the Alzheimer's brain? I don't think so, and in her paper Jie does not claim it does. Jie's point can fairly be made, but the *WSJ* [*Wall Street Journal*] article portrays it out of balance. . . .

I think before claiming that there's a sort of conspiracy of the establishment going on, one should look at the whole field in balance.

Your invoking the HIV debate strikes me as coincidental. We recently organized a Live Discussion around an article in the Journal of Medical Ethics *by a South African ethicist. He asked whether scientists have a responsibility to resist taking their internal disagreements to the general public when there's a public health interest at stake. He quoted an example that has led to disastrous public health policy in South Africa. This is an extreme case, and drugs proved clearly who was right and who was wrong, but we wanted to invite the AD field to use it as an opportunity for some navel-gazing.*

The major difference is that for HIV, it's clear who is wrong, whereas with amyloid there is no proof. My main concern is that if you think the amyloid hypothesis is wrong, then you should come up with an alternative, testable idea. Not something vague like Alzheimer's is a disease of aging, or you have too much or too little oxygen. It must be testable.

Do you consider any areas outside of the amyloid hypothesis particularly promising?

Yes. For one, the whole tau area. If one were able to block tangle formation or resolve existing tangles, that would be great. Second, the entire area of inflammation in Alzheimer's disease. That's a convoluted field, but it may play a role. Third, interventions at the level of cholesterol. Both with inflammation and cholesterol, there may be reasons to tie them into the amyloid pathway. But then again, maybe they're not tied into the amyloid pathway at all. I think either could potentially lead to treatment breakthroughs even before any anti-amyloid drug has been tested in phase 3.

Because drugs already exist?

Yes. Another area—and I don't know how fruitful it is at this point—is ApoE [a gene linked to Alzheimer's]. My personal impression is that more than 10 years after its role in AD has been discovered, we still don't understand at the molecular level how ApoE4 increases your risk of getting the disease. I think that would be an area to learn something.

I've covered ApoE extensively, and there are almost as many suggested mechanisms as labs working on it, which is not very many. Like with inflammation or cholesterol changes, some labs study the role of ApoE within the context of the amyloid hypothesis, and others look at it outside of it, but none has really hit a home run yet in any way that I can see.

Light micrograph of senile plaques show amyloid core in a brain with Alzheimer's disease. **(Martin M. Rotker/Photo Researchers, Inc.)**

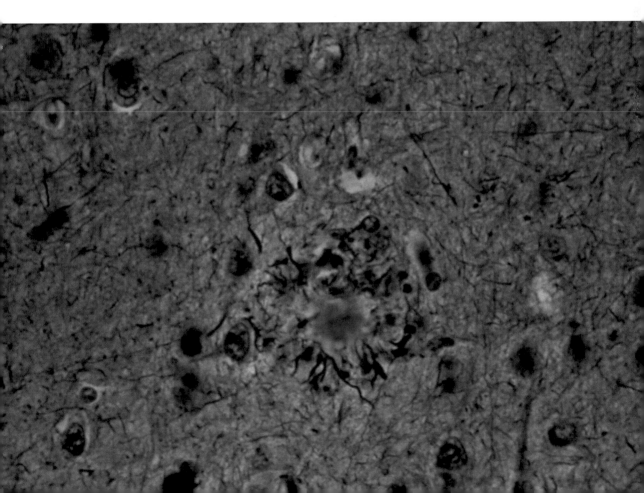

Yes. It is hard to prove anything in this field. This is why the antiinflammatories or the cholesterol-lowering drugs are so attractive. Once you can show these agents work in a clinical trial, then there will be intense motivation to find out what exactly they are doing. We have no pharmacological tool to turn ApoE4 into ApoE3. That's one of the problems in the ApoE effort. You can see a variety of effects, but to conclude which one is the key important one is very difficult.

Which facet of AD research should receive more funding than it does now?

Biomarker research. That's something companies won't touch in a major way, I think.

Why not?

Because they are focused on moving a drug forward. Researching biomarkers doesn't give you a drug per se, it just helps to make the testing of some future drugs easier. Few companies will stretch themselves for that. The likelihood of success is relatively low.

Plus companies want a drug that people take for years. Not a one-time sale.

I think the one-time diagnostic test would be interesting, but it's not a major product in itself for a company focused on drug development.

Aluminum Exposure May Increase Alzheimer's Risk

Melissa Knopper

Melissa Knopper, a contributor to *E Magazine*, writes on the possible link between aluminum exposure and increased risk of Alzheimer's disease. Knopper suggests that until scientific research on a possible aluminum-Alzheimer's link is conclusive, people should avoid daily products that contain aluminum to limit their possible aluminum exposure. She suggests that consumers look for non-aluminum-containing alternatives to items such as antiperspirants, cosmetics, and some types of cookware.

I n natural health circles, many people are tossing aluminum pans and using holistic underarm crystals instead of conventional antiperspirant. Their choices are fueled by an ongoing mystery surrounding aluminum. About 20 years ago, scientists first raised questions about a possible link between aluminum and Alzheimer's disease. Since then, researchers have gone back and forth on this

SOURCE: Melissa Knopper, "Heavy Metal?" *E Magazine: The Environmental Magazine,* vol. 16, 2005, pp. 40–63. Copyright © 2005. Reproduced with permission from *E/The Environmental Magazine.*

question. As soon as one publishes a study showing a connection, another disproves it. These days, most of the top medical experts, from the Mayo Clinic to the Alzheimer's Association, say there really is no reason to panic.

But other agencies, including the National Institute of Environmental Health Sciences (NIEHS), continue to look into it because aluminum is so ubiquitous in our daily lives. We swallow it in foods like processed cheese and baked goods. Babies encounter it in formula, breast milk and vaccines. Since aluminum is both strong and lightweight, more auto manufacturers are relying on it to boost fuel efficiency. That means more aluminum byproducts will enter the air, water and, ultimately, the landfills.

"The Alzheimer's risk with aluminum hasn't been well defined," says Robert Yokel, a University of Kentucky pharmacy professor who is studying aluminum for the NIEHS. "You have to weigh risks and benefits. My personal opinion is if you can make simple choices to avoid it until we sort this thing out, why not?"

One certainty is that Alzheimer's disease is not going away. As the baby boom generation ages and more Americans live longer, this devastating illness is affecting more patients and their families. Currently, about five percent of people over age 60 will develop Alzheimer's disease. Some research shows a relationship between aluminum and other nervous-system disorders, such as Lou Gehrig's disease and Parkinson's Disease.

Suspicious About Aluminum

Scientists first became aware of aluminum's potential health risks 20 years ago, when a group of kidney patients came down with a similar form of dementia after being exposed to aluminum through dialysis. Another study found aluminum inside the plaques and tangles that appear in Alzheimer's patients' brains.

Meanwhile, a few epidemiological studies found that people with a high level of aluminum in their drinking

A possible link has been established between aluminum exposure and increased risk of Alzheimer's disease. Suggestions have been made to cease use of aluminum cookware. (Image copyright Feng Yu, 2008. Used under license from Shutterstock.com.)

water had a higher incidence of Alzheimer's. Other studies that followed, however, did not show the same correlation. Studies of cultures that drink large amounts of tea (which leaches a lot of aluminum) also did not show a link. After several decades, scientists have been unable to replicate the original studies showing aluminum deposits in a brain affected by Alzheimer's. "There was an aluminum scare 20 years ago, but it now looks like there is no connection," says Harvard Alzheimer's researcher Dr. Ashley Bush.

New research, by Bush and others, shows Alzheimer's to be a much more complex illness than anyone had imagined. Bush's laboratory is developing a promising new drug that prevents zinc from reacting with the proteins that form the abnormal deposits in brains attacked by Alzheimer's. Phase III clinical trials of the drug, developed by Prana Biotech, will begin next year.

Experts now believe if aluminum does appear in an Alzheimer's brain, it's simply because it is so common in our environment. "It's a major component of the Earth's crust, so it shows up everywhere" Bush says. As for food and water contamination, aluminum probably isn't much of a threat because most of it passes right through the intestines without being absorbed.

Some natural health advocates disagree with this position. Suzan Walter is president of the American Holistic Health Association, and her mother died of Alzheimer's. She says many natural health experts advise patients to avoid aluminum based on the precautionary principle, and she takes steps to avoid it in her personal life. "We don't know what causes Alzheimer's, but why not stay away from aluminum just in case?" Walter asks. "It doesn't compromise my life to avoid it and it can't hurt."

Paul Schwartz, national policy coordinator for Clean Water Action, adds, "There is a valid concern to be raised about aluminum and health effects, but the science is not definitive."

Aluminum in Food and Medicine

While the metal is not easily absorbed, the government is still paying scientists like Yokel to make sure we are safe when it comes to dietary sources of aluminum. Currently, the U.S. Food and Drug Administration does not limit aluminum in food because it is "generally recognized as safe." At the same time, no one knows the exact rate the body absorbs aluminum from food. Since food accounts for 95 percent of our aluminum intake, it's worth examining, Yokel says. "We're looking into whether this constant exposure in our diet is causing a problem," Yokel says.

Yokel is also studying the rate of absorption for aluminum in drinking water. For years, municipal water treatment operators have added aluminum to their tanks to make bacteria settle out of the final product. If Yokel's ongoing experiments show our bodies absorb too much aluminum from tap water, the EPA may adopt stricter regulations.

Aluminum is so common that all of us have some background level in our bodies. For example, all mothers have traces of aluminum in their breast milk (about 40 micrograms per liter). Infant formula has about five times as much aluminum as breast milk (soy formula has the most). And the load just builds from there as a person ages.

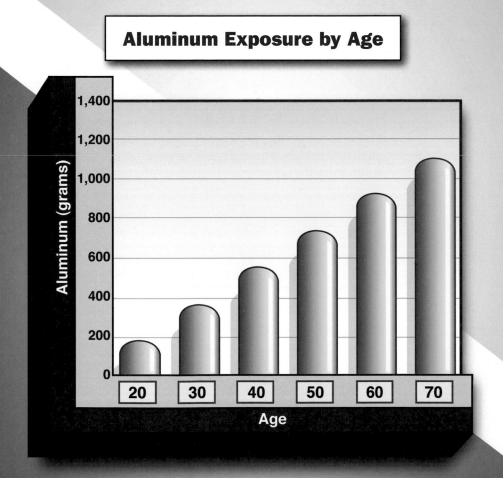

Aluminum Exposure by Age

Taken from: Alpha Omega Labs.

"If aluminum does cause Alzheimer's, it's possible that lifelong exposure could contribute," Yokel says. "Sometime later in life, you could hit that threshold and develop a problem—but it's all speculation at this point."

Certain over-the-counter medicines are loaded with aluminum. For example, the World Health Organization estimates antacid users swallow as much as five grams of aluminum per day. Buffered aspirin also has aluminum.

Vaccines are another little-known source of aluminum in our lives. The media has focused a great deal on mercury in childhood vaccines. But many vaccines also contain aluminum as an additive. That may be a concern because the body absorbs injected aluminum more easily. Vaccine critics also question whether mercury and aluminum might have a synergistic effect on the developing nervous system.

Aluminum is an important part of vaccines, however, because it makes them work better, says Dr. Paul Offit, chief of infectious diseases at the Children's Hospital of Philadelphia. "It's used when you want to enhance the immune response," Offit says. The Hepatitis B, tetanus and DPT vaccines contain aluminum, as do some batches of the flu shot.

Some parent groups, such as the Virginia-based National Vaccine Information Center, have been critical of the government's childhood vaccine policies. They argue medical policy makers and drug companies should offer vaccines without additives like mercury and aluminum.

While most childhood vaccines no longer contain mercury, aluminum might be harder to replace, says FDA spokesperson Lenore Geib. So far, no one has identified a safe alternative that can perform the same way. Even if researchers find a new substance, the testing and approval process would take years, she adds.

In pockets of the country, fears about these additives are causing an anti-vaccine backlash. Some parents are home schooling their kids to avoid government-mandated vaccines. And what about elderly patients who might skip their flu shot because they don't want an extra load of aluminum in their brains?

Offit believes the immediate benefits of vaccines outweigh any future risks. Right now, we have no definite proof that aluminum causes Alzheimer's, Offit argues. But each year, thousands of children and elderly people die of flu complications. "There is nothing theoretical about the flu," he says.

What About Antiperspirants?

Adults and teens who use antiperspirant every morning get another daily dose of aluminum. While the skin absorbs a very small percentage of the aluminum in antiperspirants, studies show, natural health advocates raise questions about the effects of constant exposure. Antiperspirants work by plugging sweat glands with aluminum salts.

Plenty of herbal alternatives are on the market at health food stores. But Yokel encourages shoppers to do their homework. A check of the label on one brand of crystal deodorant stone showed "alum" in the ingredients. That, Yokel advises, is simply a natural form of aluminum. Another option is to buy conventional deodorant, which should be aluminum-free as long as it doesn't say "antiperspirant" on the label.

Reducing Your Aluminum Intake and Alzheimer's Risk

To cut your aluminum intake, follow these steps:

- Switch to stainless steel cookware (nonstick types have other toxins).
- Try aluminum-free deodorant.
- Reduce your consumption of tea, processed cheese, and aluminum-containing baking powder.
- When possible, breastfeed. Soy formula has the most aluminum.
- Invest in a water filter.

Dr. Robert Griffith, editor of the Santa Fe–based web journal Health and Age, shares a few of the latest ideas in Alzheimer's prevention:

- Anything that is good for the heart is good for Alzheimer's, Griffith says, so keep your cholesterol low and cut calories, especially those that come from fat;
- A recent study showed walking every day cuts Alzheimer's risk;
- Take antioxidants and Vitamin C and E together. Studies show these supplements appear to have a protective effect for those at risk for Alzheimer's disease;
- Consider the herb curcumin, which may help prevent Alzheimer's;
- Eat more fruits and vegetables: they are full of antioxidants.

There Is No Strong Link Between Aluminum and Alzheimer's

Alzheimer's Society

While some claim that research linking aluminum exposure and Alzheimer's risk is conflicting or not yet decisive, the following fact sheet by the Alzheimer's Society of the United Kingdom asserts that there is no demonstrated, strong link between the daily use of everyday products containing small amounts of aluminum and increased Alzheimer's risk. The Alzheimer's Society is the largest Alzheimer's disease advocacy and information organization in the United Kingdom. It frequently provides information sheets as a public service for general audiences as well as for Alzheimer's patients and their caregivers.

A number of environmental factors have been put forward as possible contributory causes of Alzheimer's disease in some people. Among these is aluminium.

There is circumstantial evidence linking this metal with Alzheimer's disease but no causal relationship has yet been proved. As evidence for other causes continues

SOURCE: "Facts about Dementia: Aluminum and Alzheimer's Disease," Alzheimer's Society, June 2002. Reproduced by permission.

to grow, a possible link with aluminium seems increasingly unlikely.

This information sheet looks at the circumstantial evidence and current medical and scientific views. Researchers believe that, in the majority of those affected, Alzheimer's disease results from a combination of different risk factors rather than a single cause. Such factors, which vary from person to person, may include age,

Increasing Prevalence of Alzheimer's Disease (By Decades in U.S. From 1900–2050)

This graph shows how many Americans over age 65 have suffered from Alzheimer's as well as a projection of how many are likely to develop Alzheimer's through 2050.

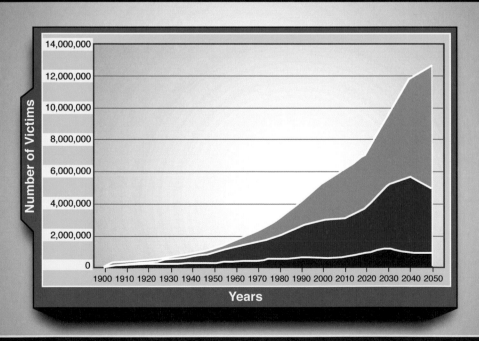

Age 66–74 Years   Age 75–84 Years   Age 85+ Years

Taken from: "Diseases Studied FAQ," *Folding@home*, Stanford University, 2007.
http://folding.stanford.edu/English/FAQ–Diseases.

genetic predisposition, other diseases or environmental agents.

The chief symptoms of Alzheimer's disease are progressive decline of memory and other higher mental functions. These changes are associated with the loss of brain cells and the development of two kinds of microscopic damage in the brain—the so-called plaques and tangles. Plaques consist of an abnormal deposit of a particular protein called beta amyloid between the brain cells. Tangles occur within cells and are formed from abnormal thread-like deposits of a protein called tau, which is normally part of the cell's 'skeleton'.

Evidence Linking Aluminium and Alzheimer's Disease

The 'aluminium hypothesis' was first put forward in 1965 when it was shown that the injection of aluminium compounds into rabbits caused tangle-like formations in nerve cells. However, these experimental tangles differ in structure and composition from Alzheimer tangles and the human brain.

Since then a number of other circumstantial links between aluminium and Alzheimer's disease have been claimed. Aluminium has been shown to be associated with both plaques and tangles in the Alzheimer brain. Some groups have disputed these claims and, in any case, the presence of aluminium does not prove a causal relationship—it is more likely to be a harmless secondary association.

It has been claimed that the brain content of aluminium is increased in Alzheimer's disease. However, recent studies in which Alzheimer brains were carefully compared with normal brains failed to find any difference in the overall amount of aluminium.

Various investigations have suggested that Alzheimer's disease is more common in areas where the aluminium content in water supplies is highest, but the method and results of these studies have been questioned. In any case, the amount of aluminium present in water supplies is minute compared with other dietary sources.

Studies of other sources of aluminium such as tea, antacid medications and antiperspirants have also failed to show a positive association with Alzheimer's disease.

People with kidney failure are unable to excrete aluminium and yet they frequently have to be treated with compounds that contain aluminium. Studies of the brains of such patients have shown that aluminium accumulates in nerve cells that are particularly vulnerable in Alzheimer's disease. However, even after years of high exposure to aluminium, patients with kidney failure do not develop dementia or the hallmark pathological changes of Alzheimer's disease.

Treatment with desferrioxamine (DFO), a drug which binds aluminium and removes it from body tissues, has been reported to slow down the mental decline in patients with Alzheimer's disease. However, the effect is small, the drug has to be given by injection into muscle and it also has a major effect on iron stores in the body. Since there is evidence that iron is involved in age-related 'oxidative' damage to tissues, the effects of DFO may have nothing to do with aluminium.

There have been many experimental studies on animals and on isolated cells showing that aluminium has toxic effects on the nervous system, but in almost all cases the doses of aluminium used were much higher than those occurring naturally in tissues.

Sources of Aluminium

The main sources of environmental aluminium are:

Food—many foods contain small amounts of aluminium.

Packaging—food may come into contact with aluminium through packaging or using aluminium foil or trays for freezing, storing or cooking. However, the amount of aluminium added to food in this way is usually negligible.

Pans—cooking in uncoated aluminium utensils can increase the amount of aluminium in certain foods such as fruits which are high in acid. Cooking foods in coated, non-stick or hard anodised aluminium pans adds virtually no aluminium to food.

Medicines—many antacids used for treating indigestion contain large amounts of aluminium compounds but normally little of the aluminium is absorbed.

Water—aluminium is naturally present in some water and, in addition, aluminium sulphate is widely used in the treatment of public water supplies. However, intake of aluminium from water is very small in comparison with other sources.

Some studies of such sources of aluminum as tea, antacids, and antiperspirants have not shown a positive association with Alzheimer's disease. **(Image copyright Graca Victoria, 2008. Used under license from Shutterstock.com.)**

Air—some aluminium from the air may enter the lungs as dust but this form is highly insoluble and hardly any reaches the rest of the body.

Only a minute proportion of the aluminium we ingest from these various sources is absorbed by the body, and even this small fraction is usually excreted in the urine or harmlessly deposited in bone which acts as a 'sink' to remove aluminium.

So effective are these mechanisms that it is estimated that the adult human body contains 30–50mg of aluminium— far less than the amount in a single antacid tablet!

The Expert View on Aluminium

There have been numerous conferences on aluminium and health ever since the idea that the metal might be a risk factor for Alzheimer's disease was first proposed. The medical research community, international and government regulatory agencies and the aluminium industry all review the evidence at frequent intervals.

The overwhelming medical and scientific opinion is that the findings outlined above do not convincingly demonstrate a causal relationship between aluminium and Alzheimer's disease, and that no useful medical or public health recommendations can be made, at least at present.

It has proved extremely difficult to devise studies which could resolve this problem one way or another. Alzheimer's is a common disease with multiple causes, while aluminium is widespread in the environment and there are no methods that allow us to measure an individual's 'body burden' or lifetime exposure to this element.

It is possible that suitable 'transgenic' animal models which develop the pathological features of Alzheimer's disease in their brains will enable scientists to determine if such changes are accelerated or exacerbated by aluminium at levels which correspond to normal human exposure.

CHAPTER 3

Patients and Caregivers Coping with Alzheimer's Disease

A Patient's Reflections on Advanced Alzheimer's

Thomas DeBaggio

Nursery owner, author, and Alzheimer's patient Thomas DeBaggio has written extensively on his battle with Alzheimer's in *When It Gets Dark* and *Losing My Mind.* He is also the subject of an occasional feature on National Public Radio chronicling his life with Alzheimer's. DeBaggio once said that having Alzheimer's was "the closest thing to being eaten alive slowly." In an April 12, 2007, NPR interview, DeBaggio's wife, Joyce, stated that Thomas could no longer write and needed help with many daily tasks. The following excerpt from his second book, *When It Gets Dark,* reflects DeBaggio's increasing struggles with memory and his continued attempts to grapple with how the disease has altered his family's life.

Photo on previous page. Alzheimer's patient Dorothy Eckert hugs her daughter Louise at their home. **(AP Images)**

I have become emotional and find tears on my cheeks when I least expect them. Tears come without warning, choking speech. Things I cannot find quickly grow into uncontrollable explosions. The world is slipping from my grasp. Frustration is abundant and I am filled with anxiety.

Squeaky floorboards speak to me in the guttural language of Hades.

The powerful winter wind tickles me as it rattles storm windows.

My most recent deficit occurred a few days ago. As I was reading, I found it difficult to understand a word. I recognized the letters but they did not mean anything; my vocabulary shrinks every day. This is why I call Alzheimer's the slow incremental death. It is so quiet and subtle it goes almost unnoticed.

I awoke this morning full of panting anxiety, unable to remember whether I am supposed to meet Dan and Tom at the Loudoun farm or at the house in Arlington.

Yet, after all this, I can still remember why there is a pile of ice bags on the porch. The bags were put there for my birthday party January 5. It was such a party, packed with old friends and new, that I don't think I will ever forget it. At the least I want to be reminded of it. It was the best thing I can remember and I have [my wife] Joyce to thank for it all, along with my friend Rick Tag and my sister, Mary Ann, and her large, useful family.

A Walk on a Winter Afternoon

No matter good or bad, I am descending into another world, full of unknown streets which I will not be able to describe for you.

> The sun arose this morning through a streaked sky etched with blood. Above empty streets the wind was brisk, and loneliness was as palpable as the screaming cold. I sit here wondering which way the words will blow.

As I turned the corner and started the last leg of my afternoon walk, I admired the emptiness of the streets. So empty were they I could easily leave the sidewalk and meander down the middle of the street, past the empty bus

An adult son walks with his senior father in the park. Alzheimer's alters the lives of families of people diagnosed with the disease. (Image copyright Lisa F. Young, 2008. Used under license from Shutterstock.com.)

parked along the road waiting for ghost riders or for the time to leave and start another round-robin of boredom behind the wheel. These ghost streets are dry and kicked by debris with the smell of cold emptiness.

I was about three quarters of the way home when the chills began to weasel their way through the many layers of clothing I had wrapped around me to keep me warm. I looked to my right as I started to cross a street. Coming down the middle of a furtive street comes a tall man

PERSPECTIVES ON DISEASES AND DISORDERS

with a large gait, walking quickly. Over his shoulders he drapes a large, colorful blanket flowing around him. He bounces with his quick gait.

The man has several days of whiskers decorating his face, and he looks like he has spent a bitterly cold night over a warm heat grate along the underground Metro line. His long, tangled hair and dirty clothes mark him as a saint of winter, one of the few souls who had left the crowded shelter. The leftover smile across his active face shines in the bitter cold. This morning a strange figure blew down a winter street on the fifth day of January 2001.

Sometimes I shut my eyes and I see, not darkness, but unknown men and women standing before a house, captured in a stiff photo of long ago. I recognize none of the faces staring with fresh smiles. Why can't I remember who they are? Did I ever know them with any intimacy, or are they shards of memory, damaged and abandoned to die?

> Torn papers and rusty leaves dance down the sidewalks
> as I walk through a winter morning, whipped by cold,
> unsteady breezes.

My Guardian

My cat Sabina possesses electric eyes that stare out of the dark bedroom, an aberration from another planet with a steady green/yellow gaze. This little cat with the thick misty coat of gray is my guardian since I fell under the control of Alzheimer's. It was at that time she came in the dark night bedroom and sat at the end of my bed, a sentinel to protect me from other deadly marauders hovering over me at night when I was helplessly asleep. She watches the door with intensity as a thin strip of light insinuates its way into the bedroom like a silent thief.

Sabina took up guarding me soon after she recovered from near death at the hands of a clumsy veterinarian. Joyce and I nursed her back to the living from trembling fear. Those were frightening days when Sabina was on the edge of death. When she recovered, she took to sleeping on my bed at night. I like to think she is paying me back now that I suffer under the death knell, waiting for Alzheimer's to slip through the thin, dark night and steal me away to the place of hot ashes and emptiness.

> There are days during which I am happier than ever, full of real joy, despite the slow death unwinding itself inside my brain.

The Nights Are Empty

At night, in the silent darkness, I lie down on the sofa and place myself carefully to see airplanes coasting in the darkness as they settle like fairies into National Airport several miles away.

To me, from where I watch, the planes are more than lights twinkling like fast-moving stars lumbering toward a landing. From where I lie in watch, I lose sight of them quickly. There is often a steady march of these silent wingless lights following their downward trajectories, but I am never able to view a landing from my sofa.

My nights are empty, as are my days, waiting here for the end to come. Apart from the moments of movement in the night air, there is only the deadly flickering of the television to comfort me.

In the depth of winter I watch snow fill the air thickly. The day is gray and forbidding, but the snow brings a festive feel and my heart beats rapidly with happiness. There is nothing I like better than a walk in a snow shower, and time to forget.

A Changing Landscape

Our house on Ivy Street has the look of a wild forgotten place. Weeds wander where there were once graveled walks. In the outdoor garden beds, the once lovely, well-tended plants are besieged by uninvited growth. The place does not sparkle as it did in earlier years. It is now full of the secrets of dying. The empty landscape is the victim of time and the people who brought change.

In earlier times, the house was bright and neat. In the backyard, a manicured garden produced red tomatoes, green and gold peppers, sassy sorrel, sweet lavenders, aromatic thymes and pungent rosemary. The cherry tree that was only a sapling when it first occupied this land is now a rough, dark, dead obelisk, slowly rotting on the spot from which it sprang many years ago.

A large greenhouse covers most of the backyard. Today it slumbers in the sun, shaded by trembling bamboo, now taller than a two-story house. A former next-door neighbor planted this out-of-context green nuisance years ago in an unsuccessful effort to thwart my dream of becoming an urban farmer. He thought the bamboo's heavy shadow created so much shade my plants would fail.

He watched as [my son] Francesco and I spent a summer digging a deep ditch the length of the property, three feet deep in heavy clay soil. We installed a heavy weed barrier on our side of his fence to stop the fickle penetration of his bamboo into our lives.

Inside the greenhouse, a sense of loss highlighted with tattooed memories stretches to meet the midday sun. Dead and dying plants lie in the deep shadows under the heavy wire benches. The place is in decline, as is its owner, and fresh weeds cover the pebbled earth.

This large greenhouse is no longer used. It is emptied of questions and laughter that filled it when the plant business was bustling. Now I am sick, weary and full of uncertainty. I am possessed by stuttering dreams and lackadaisical memory.

Yesterday has no meaning anymore. Events of today flee from memory before day concludes. My brain is full of forgotten memories. The few remaining memories are

> **FAST FACT**
>
> Over 70 percent of people with Alzheimer's disease live at home. Friends and family provide over three-quarters of their care.

scars of long ago. I live in the moment now. I remember I had a past but it is vacant now in a time of sorrow.

Falling Through the Wet Darkness

Alzheimer's is a deadly hole in my life, a deep cistern into which I tripped unknowingly. I am spinning out of control as I fall through the wet darkness. When I hit the water, I begin to sink to the bottom where the abyss greets me. I sit still, waiting for the moment I can no longer breathe.

Time is coming apart in my rough hands. An end begins to circle me. Let me hug this woman, my wife who has stood beside me for so many trembling years. I salute my son with a hug this one last time before darkness comes. Goodbye, Joyce. So long, Francesco.

Confronting Death

On dark streets it is difficult to see the faces of those walking past, especially on cold blustery days with yanked-down hats and toasty mufflers. On clear summer days the fear of death is sometimes palpable, running down sunburned cheeks.

The fear of death is everywhere, but unseen. It is under the coats of those stiff-faced, mysterious people who populate the sidewalks as they leave work. A glut of fear inhabits the soft places where no one wants to look. A man like me is appointed to excavate these sly places as he lopes toward death.

Death is a challenge for beings who can feel their own demise squirming in a deteriorating body. After you feel death crawling inside, and watch it scamper over hallucinating dark night walls, there is no reason to have fear. In the end, death does not matter; it lightens the earth's load, and enriches those who follow.

Caring for a Parent with Alzheimer's

Kathy Gade Whirity

Most Alzheimer's patients rely on family members for help with daily tasks. From providing shelter to administering in-home medical care, family caregivers act simultaneously as companions, guardians, nurses, assistants, and loved ones. Author Kathy Gade Whirity recalls the sadness of caring for her Alzheimer's-afflicted father and the difficulty of finally placing him in a long-term-care facility. She asserts that there were moments of tenderness and grace in the midst of her father's deterioration. Whirity contributed the following essay to the companion volume of *Finding the Joy in Alzheimer's*, a best-selling compilation of family and caregiver stories.

Like so many other middle-aged women, I didn't fully understand the devastating effects of Alzheimer's disease until my father was diagnosed with it. I'd read articles and personal stories dealing with this mind-stealing illness, but nothing prepared me for

SOURCE: Kathy Gade Whirity, *Finding the Joy in Alzheimer's: When Tears Are Dried with Laughter,* Pearblossom, CA: North Star Books, 2003.

actually living with the gut-wrenching emotions Alzheimer's brings to a family.

The signs were subtle at first. Dad would completely forget what he was talking about in mid-sentence. Then it progressed into Dad getting lost going to the neighborhood grocery store. My brothers, sister, and I went about our busy lives figuring that if Mom wasn't too concerned about it, we shouldn't be either. After all, we reasoned, Dad was seventy. We had to accept the fact that he was getting old.

When Mom died after a brief illness we were forced to take notice of Dad's increasingly strange behavior, which was now out of control.

Becoming a "Parent to Your Parent"

It's emotionally heartbreaking to become a parent to your own parent; to lose a father but gain a child, which is what happens when Alzheimer's comes into your life.

Dad had traveled a million *accident-free* miles throughout his career as a truck driver. An award for this proud accomplishment hung over his bed. It was now our responsibility to tell a man who had steered some of the largest semis around the city that he could no longer drive his car around the neighborhood. But, that's just what we had to do. I soon found myself relating to the helplessness other middle-aged children left taking care of a parent whose mind was faltering.

Inevitably, the time came when we had no choice but to place Dad in a nursing home after he almost burned down the kitchen. We were faced with the stark reality that this was where he belonged—for his own safety as well as our sanity. I was just beginning to find out that making the transition to becoming my father's keeper would not be an easy one.

On that first day at the nursing home, I felt the same queasy feeling I had when my daughter began her first

> **FAST FACT**
>
> Unpaid family caregivers of Alzheimer's patients gave the United States a total estimated economic asset of $83 billion in 2005.

day of kindergarten. On that long ago day, I had wanted to hug her and take her back home with me. Instead, I hid my tears and encouraged her to join the rest of the kids at play. I found it just as emotional leaving Dad behind in the strange confines of the nursing home.

As an orderly attached electronic bracelets to Dad's wrists, I sadly realized that my father would never be free again—mentally or physically. It was hard watching Dad live out the rest of his life trapped in a living purgatory, not really here, not really gone.

Coping with the Loss of Freedom

Dad suffered with Alzheimer's for about six years before his death finally set him free. But truthfully, even though I lost my father, as I had known him, many years before his death, I was also fortunate to see a side of him I might never have experienced had it not been for Alzheimer's.

There were tender moments when he'd touch my cheek and call me by name. I'd feel so elated that he had recognized me, though I knew the moment would be fleeting. I was surprised to realize that this debilitating disease could teach me life's lessons. These sentiments wouldn't be lost on me anytime soon.

I remember seeing a man's integrity in action, even though the frail, delicate frame of an old man had replaced his once strong physique. I'd watch as Dad stood at the nurses' station inquiring about a job. "I can work," he'd tell anyone who would listen. He was never the type to take something for nothing, which is why he felt it so important to pay for his meals.

Patients Reliving Old Memories

I noticed during my visits that most of the patients possessed the same admirable qualities as Dad. Honest, decent people who'd fought in wars and worked hard to give their families a better life. Young mommies who used to rock their little ones to sleep, now geriatric patients clutching

A geriatric nurse assists an elderly woman with Alzheimer's. Many children struggle with the decision to place their parents in long-term care facilities.
(© Phototake Inc./Alamy)

soft dolls to their chests as they spent their last days reliving what meant the most to them a long time ago.

Though their thin bodies were broken and their minds faded, their loving gestures were a testament that some habits born of the heart can never be broken.

I have seen countless lonely souls strolling the endless hallways of nursing homes, waiting, for the chance to connect with a warm smile, to feel the gentle touch of someone reaching out to hold their hand, or to hear a few kind words.

I've noticed that most of these older folks come alive with wide-eyed enthusiasm at the opportunity to retell stories of *the good old days*. Most cannot remember their children's names, but amazingly can recall their own childhoods as if they happened yesterday.

Dad managed to get out of the nursing home once, even though he still wore the magnetic bracelets that set off the exit alarms. He hailed a cab, and instructed the driver to take him to Canaryville, a Chicago community. He gave the address of his boyhood home, a place he'd lived more than sixty years ago.

I watched my dad grow old; his mind riddled with confusion. And yet, his soul lived in an era no disease could take away. I guess it just goes to show that no matter where the miles may take us, we always travel back to our childhood—that safe and secure place locked in our memories.

Memories Comfort Those Left to Grieve

When I received the call my father was dying I felt both panic and relief. The middle-age part of me was happy that he was finally at peace—no more confusion, no more restless agitation. But there was the little girl in me who would miss the man who could make everything okay—a man whose strength would move mountains if his family needed him to.

As I sit here, with graying hair and multiplying wrinkles, I find contentment in my own childhood memories, of a dad who chased away monsters and calmed the fears that midnight storms would sometimes bring. Because of Dad's illness, I realize that our childhood memories shall never grow old, for the emotion behind them will never lose its comfort to our souls.

Alzheimer's is like a thief in the night, ultimately stealing a person's mind. For the caregiver, however, there are lessons to be learned. If I've learned anything from this experience, it is to enjoy the precious gift of memories that I am able to share with my own daughters.

These gifts can be tucked away in a corner of their middle-aged hearts, to comfort them later, at a time when life might find them becoming a parent to me.

Coping with Caring for Alzheimer's Patients

Kim Archer

In the following viewpoint Kim Archer explains that caring for loved ones with Alzheimer's disease (AD) places significant financial, physical, and emotional burdens on caregivers, who are most likely family members of the AD patient. Archer points out that caregivers often neglect their own physical and emotional health, sometimes leading to long-term and life-threatening illnesses. Increased support for family caregivers may help alleviate their stress, fatigue, and illness. She relates the story of Debbie Clancy and her struggle to care for her Alzheimer's-afflicted mother. Archer is a staff writer for the *Tulsa World* in Oklahoma.

D ebbie Clancy remembers her mother as a vibrant woman with a love for preparing her native Lebanese specialties like tabouli and baklava.

Her mom owned a delicatessen in the 1960s in Tulsa's Harvard Village and once scolded her oldest daughter for using rubber gloves as she baked. "A cook has to feel the food," Clancy's mother told her.

SOURCE: Kim Archer, "Coping with Caring," *The Tulsa World*, December 14, 2006, p. D1. Copyright World Publishing Co., 2006. Reproduced by permission.

After a lifelong passion for food preparation, Clancy's 81-year-old mother has lost all interest in cooking. Her passion has been wiped away by Alzheimer's disease and vascular dementia.

"My mom has always cooked my whole life, but she's just not interested anymore," she said. "It's so hard because you see this gorgeous, gleaming, happy face. As much as you love and embrace them, they're kind of slipping into themselves."

Clancy is one of the many caregivers for the estimated 4.5 million people with Alzheimer's disease in this country. There are an estimated 79,000 Oklahomans with Alzheimer's disease, and likely a caregiver for each one of them. It is a job filled with uncertainty, fear, sadness and frustration.

"If I didn't have my support group, I wouldn't make it," Clancy said.

Caring for Alzheimer's-Afflicted Relatives Is a Heavy Burden

According to a survey by the National Alliance for Caregiving and the Alzheimer's Association, caregivers of people with Alzheimer's disease or other dementias shoulder a particularly heavy burden of care. The type of care these people must provide is often more emotionally and physically demanding than for other kinds of caregiving, the survey said.

In fact, studies have shown that caregivers often are so stressed from the job they get sick and die before the person with Alzheimer's disease does. "That is absolutely true. The caregiver has to start thinking for two. The stress can be immense," said JoAnn Webster, early onset coordinator for the Oklahoma and Arkansas chapter of the Alzheimer's Association.

Alzheimer's disease is a progressive disease of the brain that causes problems with memory, thinking and behavior that are not a normal part of aging, she said.

Caregivers Adjust to New Roles

Many factors make the disease difficult on the caregiver, especially the role change that happens when caring for a loved one with Alzheimer's disease. "If a breadwinner has the disease, that can completely change the roles in the couple's relationship," Webster said. "People with early onset of the disease may still have children at home. Or an adult child may have to care for their parent. The diagnosis can be extremely devastating to the family dynamics."

A person with Alzheimer's disease often can't remember where to find things or how to do things they used to do. Sequencing of tasks becomes confusing and, eventually, the person doesn't remember how to take baths or put on makeup. "They might take the trash outside, but leave the trash can in the drive," Webster said. "I had a caregiver bring in his wife's cosmetics, and we marked them so she would know what to put on when. The caregiver is constantly trying to simplify tasks."

Caregivers Need Support

In turn, caregivers often neglect their own care. Caregivers often don't eat right or sleep well. They may have hypertension or ulcers that go untreated, conditions exacerbated by the stress of caregiving, she said.

"That's where we say, 'We can help. Call us,'" Webster said. "Support groups are wonderful. You talk with people who've been there, done that and gotten their T-shirt." The Alzheimer's Association offers many support programs, including counseling for caregivers and in-home consultations.

Debbie Clancy sees the group's services as a lifeline. "I've learned so much. I have a kind of perspective on the disease I didn't have before. I've gotten ideas I can use," she said. She has learned that when her mother is frustrated or confused, she may lash out at Clancy, a common symptom of Alzheimer's disease. Often those times come when Clancy's mother feels her independence is threatened.

This peaceful room in a care facility is filled with soft changing colors and sounds from nature. It helps calm patients without the use of drugs, enabling caregivers to concentrate on patients' other concerns. (**AP Images**)

"The worst battles have constantly been about the car," she said. Her mother sometimes asks Clancy to drive her somewhere. But when frustrated, Clancy's mother threatens to drive herself. "Just this morning, Mom insisted she would drive herself where she wanted to go. She can't drive because she has seizures," she said. "For the person with the illness, they feel as if you're taking their freedom away. But I'm not. It's kind of an inner battle."

Caregivers Face Constant Challenges

Two years ago, Clancy asked her mother to take her medication. In frustration, her mother threw the pills across the room. Clancy bit her tongue as her 2-year-old grandson looked on. He saw Clancy's face, swirled around and pointed his finger at Clancy's mother and said, "You better behave."

"He read me. He was brilliant," she said. Feeling the stress rising inside, Clancy left the room. Fifteen minutes later, Clancy returned to find her mother had picked up her pills and was calm. "I've learned not to take it personally because it's not. I don't argue and I don't confront," she said.

Clancy said she is lucky her mother lives next door in her own house. Yet she is concerned her mom might wander away, a common problem among people with Alzheimer's disease.

Webster said she recently knew of a man with Alzheimer's disease who set out to drive to his local bank. But when he tried to return home, he got confused. He got on Interstate 44 and ended up in Missouri. "He had a credit card in his pocket, and he just drove. They tracked him down 36 hours later," she said.

That hasn't yet been a problem for Clancy. "I do get concerned. There are options out there so that when the time comes, I can protect her. At this point, I don't need it," she said.

In advanced cases, Webster said the person with Alzheimer's disease may no longer be able to identify the caregiver. This can be particularly troubling to the caregiver who may be a longtime spouse or adult child.

FAST FACT

Almost 10 million Americans are caring for a person with Alzheimer's disease or another dementia.

"They lose memory in the reverse order they learned things. They might say, 'I want to go home' or 'I want my mama,'" she said. "That can be very disconcerting for a caregiver."

"But what the person with Alzheimer's is saying is that home was a secure place. Often, it's more of a statement that 'I am afraid. I don't understand what is going on,'" Webster said.

Clancy's mother hasn't exhibited that level of memory loss.

Internet Resources Help Caregivers Prepare for the Future

"I think the most helpful thing to me has been the caregiver's checklist," Clancy said. The list provides tips on dealing with the special needs of a person with Alzheimer's disease.

"I think it's prepared me for what to expect," Clancy said. Eventually, people with Alzheimer's disease need around-the-clock care. "Until that time comes, it can be a very difficult road," Webster said.

On a recent Saturday afternoon, Clancy was able to coax her mother into making some of her traditional holiday treats, from baklava to pretzels and Syrian cookies. "She's always cooked. I learned from the best," Clancy said. "I'm just going to love her every minute I have her."

Caretakers Deal with Grief

Sandy Braff and Mary Rose Olenik

Staying Connected While Letting Go by Sandy Braff and Mary Rose Olenik not only chronicles the daily struggles of Alzheimer's patients and their caregivers but also supports caregivers through a long, difficult, and emotional grieving process. The following excerpt from that book illustrates family-member and caregiver frustrations with some Alzheimer's-induced behaviors, such as temper tantrums and lying. Ultimately, the caregivers and family members are compelled to confront their own denial that their loved one is changing—and ultimately dying—as a result of the disease. Since 1989 Braff, an author and licensed therapist, has conducted an Alzheimer's caregiver support group for the San Diego Alzheimer's Association. Olenik is a caregivers' advocate and author who regularly writes on issues faced by Alzheimer's patients and their caregivers.

Because of the ambiguity of the diagnosis, "possible/ probable Alzheimer's disease," many caregivers struggle with their denial. Although denial is often portrayed as negative, it can also serve a positive function. Denial can be viewed as an ally determined to protect you from confronting a painful reality until you have mustered up enough inner strength to deal with the situation. When you use a defense mechanism such as denial, for example, it is not so much that you are unaware of the reality of the diagnosis, but that when you project that reality into the future it becomes both too painful and scary for you to acknowledge at the time the diagnosis is made. When you are able to gain a sense of control and can plan, organize, and make decisions that effectively impact your future, you will become less frightened. When you acquire a sense of competence in handling both your reactions and your patient's symptoms, you will be able to transition into accepting the reality that at first overwhelmed you. Once this stage is achieved, you will then be able to let go of denial and come to terms with or meet head on the challenges of Alzheimer's disease. . . .

Veronica

Veronica's story provides an excellent example of problematic denial. Her face pale and voice strained, she spoke about her husband, Zeke's, disconcerting behavior.

We can no longer socialize with friends down at the clubhouse. I'm constantly humiliated because Zeke repeatedly asks the same questions and persists in telling the same stories. I think he is doing this to embarrass me. He never liked going to these club events anyway.

He seems to want me to do more and more for him. Sometimes he doesn't eat his dinner or he picks up his meat in his fingers. Does he expect me to feed him? Zeke will not take his medications. I put them on the counter for him. I leave notes telling him when to take them. I remind him constantly. I'm doing all of this for him, and he does diddlysquat for me. I get so worked up talking about this, it convinces me all the more that he's lazy, selfish, and feeling sorry for himself.

Spouses, children, and other family members face many challenges as they care for their loved ones with Alzheimer's. (© Photofusion Picture Library/Alamy)

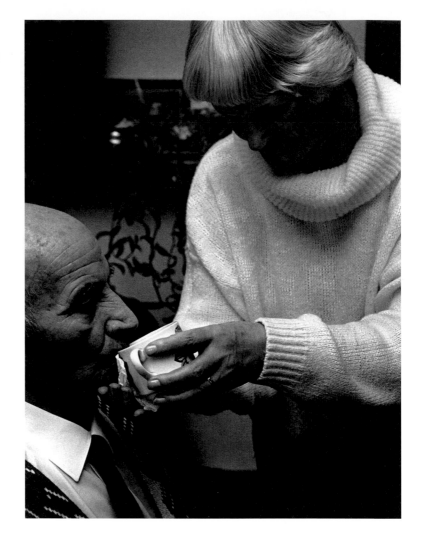

Veronica was obviously unable to accept her husband's illness, and her denial made it inevitable that she would take his behaviors personally. Her intense denial became problematic when she said she would not be responsible for giving Zeke his medication. It took several months for members of the group to help Veronica understand that her husband's behaviors were a result of a brain disease, and that he truly had a memory problem and could not be trusted to remember to take his medication without her assistance. . . .

Elizabeth

Elizabeth was a retired high school teacher who was very involved in the city council and other political activities. She had rosy cheeks, short cropped gray hair, and was very spunky and vocal. In spite of the education she received in the group about the impact of Alzheimer's disease on the brain and how it affects behavior, Elizabeth continued to struggle with her denial of the consequences of this disease on her husband, Harvey, and their reasonable lifestyle. Once again in the group meeting, she bemoaned the fact that her husband "lied" all the time. She was furious, and there was an edge to her voice as she spoke to the group.

Harvey lies all the time. The one thing I cannot tolerate is lying. He says he does not know where things are although he is the one who puts them away, and then he accuses me of hiding things and denies that he had anything to do with the lost item. It could be clothing, a book, money, anything. I just want him to tell the truth!

One of the group members, cognizant of Elizabeth's anger identifying with her denial, empathetically stated, "You just don't want him to have this disease." Other members acknowledged her statement and showed their understanding; nodding in silence. Then Elizabeth said softly, "I wish my husband would just wake up tomorrow and be the way he always was."

Elizabeth, appreciative of the group's profound understanding, implored, "Please be patient with me. This is the hardest thing I've ever done."

> ## FAST FACT
>
> One-third of primary family caregivers die before the person with Alzheimer's for whom they are caring.

Frank

Frank, a very strong, determined gentleman, was able to transcend his battle with denial and redirect his energy and passion toward more realistic and productive activities.

Frank had sold his small manufacturing business back east and retired to Southern California with his wife, Olympia, so they would be close to their two daughters and their families. He was an energetic, "take charge" kind of guy, who had confidently controlled his business and had made the major family decisions for years. Early in his wife's illness, true to his character, he believed that he could, and without a doubt would, find a way to cure her. Thus, he aggressively began his quest. Frank sent for information from a multitude of sources and networked throughout the country with various Alzheimer's disease research groups. During one of my visits, he told me he was seriously considering moving them to Texas for a few years, as there was a potential cure being offered by a research group there. However, after further investigation, he decided their results were really not plausible enough to warrant such a major change. Instead he decided to enroll Olympia in an experimental drug study at the local university.

Six months later, when I arrived at Frank's apartment, he was furious. He had just found out that Olympia had probably been on a placebo in the research study. He had also exhausted all other resources. The reality that he was not going to find a cure, because one didn't exist, and that he was not capable of restoring his wife's health, seemed to demoralize him. However, as these strong feelings dissipated, he gave himself permission to stop chasing the fantasy. Also, after adamantly denying, during this time, that a support group could be helpful, he finally decided to attend one.

By my next visit, six months later, with the same gusto by which he lived his entire life, he had become a regular member of two groups, an active advocate for caregivers, and was helping them resolve some of their legal, financial, and health insurance problems. Frank lightheartedly added that he took his anger out on the golf course and responded to his wife with a patience of which he never thought himself capable.

GLOSSARY

allele   Any of two or more alternative forms of a gene that occupy the same location on a chromosome.

alternative medicine   A term used to describe approaches to health care that are used in place of conventional medicine, including acupuncture, Chinese medicine, homeopathy, and herbal medicine.

aluminum   An extremely light, whitish, lustrous, metallic element. Excessive amounts of aluminum in the body can have a variety of toxic effects.

Alzheimer's disease   A progressive, degenerative brain disease with no known cause or cure.

ApoE   The abbreviation for apolipoprotein E, a gene that codes for a protein component of lipoproteins (complexes of fat and protein) that are normal parts of blood plasma. Some studies have indicated that ApoE may be involved in the development of Alzheimer's disease.

asymptomatic   A state in which an individual does not exhibit or experience symptoms of a disease.

ataxia   Unsteadiness in walking or standing that is associated with brain diseases.

atrophy   Decreasing in size or wasting away of a body part or tissue.

biomarker   A molecular indicator used to indicate or measure a biological process, often the progression of a disease.

blastocyst   A thin-walled hollow structure that contains a cluster of cells called the inner cell mass from which the embryo arises. A blastocyst develops about five days after fertilization.

blood clots	A clump or thickened mass of blood in an artery that may partially or completely block the flow of blood. If a blood clot dislodges it may travel through the body and cause a stroke or heart attack.
calcium	An essential mineral necessary for proper bone, nerve, and muscle formation and function.
caregiver	Someone who provides or assists with the basic care and safety needs of a person who is unable to care for him- or herself because of disease, age, or other incapacity.
case fatality rate	The rate of patients suffering disease or injury that die as a result of that disease or injury during a specific period of time.
case fatality ratio	A ratio indicating the number of persons who die as a result of a particular disease, usually expressed as a percentage or as the number of deaths per 1,000 cases.
catalyst	A substance that speeds up a chemical process without actually changing the products of reaction.
chronic fatigue syndrome (CFS)	A condition that causes debilitating fatigue that lasts for six months or longer. People with CFS also have many other symptoms, including pain in the joints and muscles, headache, and sore throat. CFS appears to result from a combination of factors.
clinical trials	A research study designed to test the safety and effectiveness of vaccines, new drugs, or new ways of using existing drugs.
Creutzfeldt-Jakob disease (CJD)	A transmissible, rapidly progressing, fatal neurodegenerative disorder related to bovine spongiform encephalopathy (BSE), commonly called mad cow disease.
CT scan	Computed tomography (CT) is an X-ray technique in which a three-dimensional image of a body part is put together by computer using a series of X-ray pictures taken from different angles along a straight line; often called computerized axial tomography (CAT) scan.
cutaneous	Pertaining to the skin.

degenerative   A condition that progressively, and often irreversibly, deteriorates over time.

dehydration   The loss of water and salts essential for normal body function. Dehydration occurs when the body loses more fluid than it takes in.

dementia   The progressive deterioration and eventual loss of mental ability that is severe enough to interfere with normal activities of daily living, lasts more than six months, is not present since birth, and is not associated with a loss or alteration of consciousness. Dementia is a group of symptoms caused by gradual death of brain cells. Dementia is usually caused by degeneration in the cerebral cortex, the part of the brain responsible for thoughts, memories, actions, and personality.

demographics   The characteristics of human populations or specific parts of human populations, most often reported through statistics.

deoxyribonucleic acid (DNA)   Deoxyribonucleic acid (DNA) is a double-stranded, helical molecule that forms the molecular basis for heredity in most organisms.

depression   A mental condition characterized by a pessimistic sense of inadequacy, sadness, and despair along with loss of energy and a despondent lack of activity.

EEG   An EEG (electroencephalogram) is a graphic recording that shows and measures the changing strength of the brain's electric field.

embryo   The earliest stage of animal development in the uterus before the animal is considered a fetus.

embryonic stem cells   Undifferentiated cells derived from embryos that may be developed into a wide variety of highly specialized cells.

enzyme   Molecules that act as critical catalysts in biological systems. Catalysts are substances that increase the rate of chemical reactions without being consumed in the reaction.

epidemic   A widespread outbreak of an infectious disease.

epidemiology   The study of the various factors that influence the occurrence, distribution, prevention, and control of disease, injury, and other health-related events in a defined human population. By the application of various analytical techniques including mathematical analysis of the data, the probable cause of an infectious outbreak can be pinpointed.

etiology   The study of the cause or origin of a disease or disorder.

gene   The fundamental physical and functional unit of heredity. Whether in a microorganism or in a human cell, a gene is an individual element of an organism's genome and determines a trait or characteristic by regulating biochemical structure or metabolic process.

gene therapy   The treatment of inherited diseases by corrective genetic engineering of the dysfunctional genes. Gene therapy is part of a broader field called genetic medicine, which involves the screening, diagnosis, prevention, and treatment of hereditary conditions in humans. The results of genetic screening can pinpoint a potential problem to which gene therapy can sometimes offer a solution.

genetic engineering   The altering of the genetic material of living cells in order to make them capable of producing new substances or performing new functions.

genetics   The study of genes and their effects on inheritance of specific traits, diseases, and other biological processes.

genome   All of the genetic information for a cell or organism.

genotype   The genetic information that a living thing inherits from its parents that affects its makeup, appearance, and function.

ginkgo biloba   An extract from the leaves of the ginkgo tree, ginkgo biloba is an alternative medicine used primarily to aid memory and concentration.

latent   A condition that is potential or dormant, not yet manifest or active.

meat packing	The wholesale slaughtering, processing, and distribution of animals for consumption by humans or other animals.
MRI	Magnetic resonance imaging (MRI) is a technique for producing computerized three-dimensional images of tissues inside the body using radio waves.
myalgia	Muscular aches and pain.
neurologist	An expert in the scientific study of the nervous system, especially its structure, functions, and abnormalities.
nutritional supplements	Substances necessary to health, such as calcium or protein, that are taken in concentrated form to compensate for dietary insufficiency, poor absorption, unusually high demand for that nutrient, or other reasons.
nv-CJD	Abbreviation for "new variant-Creutzfeldt-Jakob disease"; nv-CJD appears to be a newer form of CJD, a rapidly progressing, fatal neurodegenerative disorder related to bovine spongiform encephalopathy (BSE), commonly called mad cow disease.
pathogen	A disease-causing agent, such as a bacteria, virus, or fungus.
PET scan	A positron emission tomography (PET) scan is a radiologic imaging technique that involves the injection of radioactive dye into the body to produce three-dimensional images of the internal tissues or organs being studied.
plaque	An area of inflamed or demyelinated (a loss of protective "insulation") central nervous system tissue.
prevalence	The actual number of cases of disease (or injury) that exist in a population.
prions	Proteins that are infectious. The name prion is derived from "proteinaceous infectious particles." The discovery of prions and confirmation of their infectious nature overturned a basic notion that infections were caused only by intact organisms, particularly microorganisms such as bacteria, fungi, parasites, or viruses. The prevailing attitude was that a protein could not cause disease.

progressive disease   A disease that gets worse over time.

prophylaxis   Pre-exposure treatments (for example, immunization) that prevent or reduce severity of disease or symptoms upon exposure.

relapse   A return of symptoms after the patient has apparently recovered from a disease.

seizure   A sudden disruption of the brain's normal electrical activity accompanied by altered consciousness and/or other neurological and behavioral abnormalities.

spongiform   The clinical name for the appearance of brain tissue affected by prion diseases, such as Creutzfeld-Jakob disease or bovine spongiform encephalopathy (mad cow disease). The disease process leads to the formation of tiny holes in brain tissue, giving it a spongy appearance.

stem cell   A renewable and unspecialized cell found among specialized cells in a tissue or organ.

systemic   Any medical condition that affects the whole body.

toxic   Something that is poisonous and that can cause illness or death.

vaccination   The introduction of weakened or dead viruses or microorganisms into the body to create immunity by the production of specific antibodies. The use of vaccines is designed to prevent specific diseases within humans and animals by producing immunity to such diseases.

CHRONOLOGY

1906   Alois Alzheimer, a German neurologist and psychiatrist, first describes what would later be called Alzheimer's disease after discovering "plaques and tangles" in the brain of a patient who had suffered severe and progressive dementia.

1910   Researcher Emil Kraepelin names Alzheimer's disease after Alois Alzheimer.

1970s   Interest in Alzheimer's disease research intensifies.

1974   The National Institute on Aging is established.

1976   Biochemical changes in the brain are linked to Alzheimer's disease.

1978   The Alzheimer Society of Canada, the first Alzheimer's support organization, is established to promote research and public awareness, provide information, and aid Alzheimer's patients and caregivers.

1979   The Alzheimer's Association is founded in the United States.

1980s   Alzheimer's disease research concentrates on the causes and effects of brain plaque associated with the disease.

1992   Researchers discover a genetic link to a rare form of Alzheimer's disease.

1993   The role of the ApoE gene in the brain is identified and marked as a risk factor for Alzheimer's.

The first Alzheimer's drug becomes available. Cholinesterase inhibitors, created to lessen symptoms early in the progression of Alzheimer's disease and dementia, are approved for use.

1994   Former president Ronald Reagan announces he has Alzheimer's disease.

1996   The Alzheimer's drug Aricept is approved for use by the U.S. Food and Drug Administration (FDA).

1999   The first potential Alzheimer's disease vaccine is tested on mice.

Genetic mutations are linked to the patterned cell death of neurons.

2000   Brain imaging is used to study Alzheimer's disease.

2002   A human trial is conducted to test a potential Alzheimer's vaccine. AN-1792 is tested in humans, but the study is stopped after several volunteers experienced severe inflammation of the brain and spinal cord.

2003   Namenda becomes the first medication specifically approved to treat severe forms of Alzheimer's disease.

2004   Former president Reagan dies.

Diabetes is linked with an increased Alzheimer's risk.

The U.S. Congress hears testimony on the possible benefits of embryonic stem cell research on Alzheimer's disease.

2005 Research increases on the effects of diet, exercise, mental stimulation, stress, and vitamin intake on the risk of developing Alzheimer's disease.

2006 The National Institute on Aging launches the Alzheimer's Disease Neuroimaging Initiative (ADNI) to study Alzheimer's in eight hundred patients nationwide and search for biomarkers for the disease.

Alzheimer's Association
225 N. Michigan Ave. Ste. 1700
Chicago, IL 60611-7633
(800) 272-3900
fax: (312) 335-1110
www.alz.org

The Alzheimer's Association is a nonprofit association that supports the families and caregivers of Alzheimer's patients, promotes brain health, and advances Alzheimer's research. The association operates the Alzheimer's Association Green-Field Library, the nation's largest library dedicated to the disease. The association publishes abundant information about the disease, including the journal *Alzheimer's and Dementia*.

Alzheimer's Disease Education and Referral Center (ADEAR)
PO Box 8250
Silver Spring, MD 10907-8250
(301) 495-3311
(800) 438-4380
fax: (301) 495-3334
www.alzheimers.org

The Alzheimer's Disease Education and Referral Center distributes information in response to inquiries from health professionals, patients, caregivers, and families. Information includes current research efforts and findings, referral to treatment centers, support groups, and family support services. ADEAR is a service of the U.S. National Institute on Aging (NIA).

Alzheimer's Disease International
64 Great Suffolk St.
London SE1 0BL UK
www.alz.co.uk

Alzheimer's Disease International is an umbrella organization for nearly forty-five Alzheimer's organizations worldwide. The organization's Web site provides general information on AD and links to other Alzheimer's organizations. *Global Perspectives*, the organization's newsletter that is published three times per year, can also be found at the Web site.

Alzheimer's Foundation of America
322 8th Ave., 7th Floor
New York, NY 10001
(866) 232-8484
fax: (646) 638-1546
www.alzfdn.org

The Alzheimer's Foundation of America asserts that "no one should have to face Alzheimer's alone." The foundation provides information and support for families, caregivers, and the public. The foundation's Web site also has a dedicated section for teen relatives of Alzheimer's patients.

Alzheimer's Research Center (ARC)
Medical College of Georgia Foundation Alumni Center, FI-1003A
Augusta, GA 30912
www.mcg.edu/centers/alz/

The Alzheimer's Research Center (ARC) is a dedicated Alzheimer's research facility. Much of ARC's research occurs at its Animal Behavior Center, a state-of-the-art nonhuman primate facility of the Medical College of Georgia.

Alzheimer's Society
Gordon House
10 Greencoat Pl.
London SWlP 1PH UK
+44 (0)20-7306-0606
fax: (0)20-7306-0808
www.alzheimers.org.uk

The Alzheimer's Society is a nonprofit organization in the United Kingdom dedicated to providing information on Alzheimer's and supporting patients and families living with Alzheimer's.

AlzOnline
Alzheimer's Caregiver Support Online
State of Florida Department of Elder Affairs and the University of Florida
(866) 260-2466
www.alzonline.phhp.ufl.edu

AlzOnline is a national online education, support, and information network for caregivers and families. The organization offers numerous documents at its Web site to aid caregivers in finding services, helping the Alzheimer's patient through daily activities, and coping with stress, fatigue, and grief.

American Health Assistance Foundation's Alzheimer's Disease Research Program
15825 Shady Grove Rd., Suite 140
Rockville, MD 20850
(301) 948-3244
(800) 437-2423
fax: (301) 258-9454
www.ahaf.org

The American Health Assistance Foundation's Alzheimer's Disease Research Program provides funding for and conducts research on Alzheimer's disease. The foundation also provides educational publications and emergency financial assistance to Alzheimer's patients and their caregivers.

Centers for Disease Control and Prevention (CDC)
1600 Clifton Rd.
Atlanta, GA 30333
(404) 639-3311
www.cdc.gov

The Centers for Disease Control and Prevention (CDC) is the main health agency of the U.S. government. The mission of the CDC is to promote health and quality of life by preventing and controlling disease, injury, and disability. The CDC is the focus of the U.S. government's efforts to develop and implement prevention and control strategies for diseases. The CDC provides up-to-date information to the public on health and diseases. The agency publishes several journals, including *Emerging Infectious Diseases* and *Morbidity and Mortality Weekly Report.*

Eldercare Locator
(800) 677-1116
www.eldercare.gov

This service of the Administration on Aging, funded by the U.S. federal government, provides information on and referrals to respite care and other home and community services offered by state and area agencies.

National Institute on Aging
Public Information Office, Bldg. 31
Rm. 5C27
31 Center Dr.
MSC 2292
Bethesda, MD 20892-2292
(301) 496-1752
TYY: (800) 222-4225
www.nih.gov/nia/

A division of the U.S. National Institutes of Health (NIH), the National Institute on Aging (NIA) directs research and provides information on health issues affecting older people.

National Institutes of Health
9000 Rockville Pike
Bethesda, MD 20892
www.nih.gov

The National Institutes of Health (NIH), a division of the U.S. Department of Health and Human Services (DHHS), directs medical research in the areas of prevention, causes, treatments, and cures for diseases.

FOR FURTHER READING

Books

Elizabeth Cohen, *The House on Beartown Road: A Memoir of Learning and Forgetting.* New York: Random House, 2003.

Joanne Koenig Coste, *Learning to Speak Alzheimer's: A Groundbreaking Approach for Everyone Dealing with the Disease.* Boston: Houghton Mifflin, 2004.

B.J. FitzRay, *Alzheimer's Activities: Hundreds of Activities for Men and Women with Alzheimer's Disease and Related Disorders.* Windsor, CA: Rayve, 2001.

Bretten C. Gordeau and Jeffrey G. Hillier, *Alzheimer's Essentials.* Carma, 2005.

H. Gruetzner, *Alzheimer's: A Caregiver's Guide and Sourcebook.* New York: Wiley, 2001.

George Krause, *At Wit's End: Plain Talk on Alzheimer's for Families and Clinicians.* Purdue, IN: Purdue University Press, 2006.

Daniel Kuhn, *Alzheimer's Early Stages: First Steps for Families, Friends and Caregivers.* Alameda, CA: Hunter House, 2003.

Nancy L. Mace, *The 36-Hour Day: A Family Guide to Caring for Persons with Alzheimer Disease, Related Dementing Illnesses, and Memory Loss in Later Life.* 3rd ed. New York: Warner, 2006.

Mayo Clinic, *Mayo Clinic Guide to Alzheimer's Disease.* Rochester, MN: Mayo Clinic, 2006.

Stephen G. Post, *The Moral Challenge of Alzheimer Disease: Ethical Issues from Diagnosis to Dying.* Baltimore: Johns Hopkins University Press, 2000.

L.S. Powell, *Alzheimer's Disease: A Guide for Families and Caregivers.* Cambridge, MA: Perseus, 2002.

Richard Taylor, *Alzheimer's from the Inside Out.* Health Professions Press, 2003.

PERSPECTIVES ON DISEASES AND DISORDERS

Rosette Teitel, *The Handholder's Handbook: A Guide to Caregivers of People with Alzheimer's or Other Dementias.* New Brunswick, NJ: Rutgers University Press, 2001.

Periodicals

Catherine Arnst. "'I Can't Remember,'" *Business Week Online*, August 22, 2003.

Christine Gorman, Alice Park, Kristina Dell, and Dan Cray, "The Fires Within," *Time*, vol. 163, no. 8, February 23, 2004.

Megan Othersen Gorman, "Now, There's New Hope for Alzheimer's," *Prevention*, vol. 54, no. 1, January 2002.

GP, "Copper Implicated in Alzheimer's," November 9, 2007.

Jane Gross, "Living with Alzheimer's Before a Window Closes," *New York Times*, March 29, 2007.

Houston Chronicle (Houston, TX), "Poignant Romance Blooms for O'Connor's Husband," November 14, 2007.

Claudia Kalb and Debra Rosenberg, "Nancy's Next Campaign," *Newsweek*, June 21, 2004.

Barbara Kantrowitz, Karen Springen, and Anne Underwood, "Confronting Alzheimer's," *Newsweek*, June 18, 2007.

Medicine & Health, "A Blood Test Could Hold the Key to Predicting Alzheimer's Disease: Tests in This Study Proved 90 and 92 Percent Accurate," vol. 61, no. 41, November 2, 2007.

Newsweek, "The Aging Brain; Old Genes, New Findings," January 17, 2005.

———, "Stronger, Faster, Smarter," March 26, 2007.

Alice Park, "What You Can Do," *Time*, vol. 163, no. 8, February 23, 2004.

Andrew Pollack, "Scientists Report Advances in Diagnosing Alzheimer's Years Before Onset," *New York Times*, October 15, 2007.

PR Newswire, "Groundbreaking ApoE Gene Diet Linked to Alzheimer's Disease and Heart Disease Prevention," November 6, 2007.

N. Seppa, "Looking for Biomarkers: Protein Signature May Warn of Impending Alzheimer's Disease," *Science News*, vol. 172, no. 16, October 20, 2007.

Internet Sources

Alzheimer's Association, "The Basics of Alzheimer's," 2005. www.alz.org/national/documents/brochure_basicsofalz_low.pdf.

Area Agency on Aging, "Caregiver's Checklist," 2007. www.agingcarefl.org/caregiver/alzheimers/checklist.

Guide to Long Term Care, "Could It Be Alzheimer's? The 10 Possible Early Warning Signs," 2004. http://guidetolongtermcare.com/alzheimers.html.

MedlinePlus, Alzheimer's Disease," 2007. www.nlm.nih.gov/medlineplus/alzheimersdisease.html.

National Center for Health Statistics, CDC, "Alzheimer's Disease—Statistics," 2006. www.cdc.gov/nchs/fastats/alzheimr.htm.

INDEX